PERFORMANCE

An Alphabet of Performative Writing

Ronald J. Pelias

Walnut Creek, California

LEFT COAST PRESS, INC.
1630 North Main Street, #400
Walnut Creek, CA 94596
www.LCoastPress.com

ISBN 978-1-61132-286-6 hardback
ISBN 978-1-61132-287-3 paperback
ISBN 978-1-61132-288-0 institutional eBook
ISBN 978-1-61132-289-7 consumer eBook

Library of Congress Cataloging-in-Publication Data
Pelias, Ronald J.
Performance : an alphabet of performative writing / Ronald J Pelias.
pages cm
Summary: "Performance uses the alphabet as an organizational device to present a series of short pieces that approach performance from multiple perspectives and various compositional strategies. Pelias's essays, poetry, dialogue, personal narratives, quick speculations, and other literary genres explore the key themes in this field, encapsulating the essence of performance studies for the novice and providing food for thought for the expert. Its brief, evocative, and reflexive pieces introduce performative writing as a method of research for those in performance and many other fields"—Provided by publisher.
Includes bibliographical references.
ISBN 978-1-61132-286-6 (hardback)—ISBN 978-1-61132-287-3 (paperback)—ISBN 978-1-61132-288-0 (institutional eBook)—ISBN 978-1-61132-289-7 (consumer eBook)
1. Performing arts—Philosophy. 2. Creation (Literary, artistic, etc.) I. Title.
PN1584.P385 2014
790.201—dc23
2013041742

Printed in the United States of America

∞™ The paper used in this publication meets the minimum requirements of American National Standard for Information Sciences—Permanence of Paper for Printed Library Materials, ANSI/NISO Z39.48–1992.

Contents

Beginnings

1
A Familiar Framing

Performance: An Alphabet of Performative Writing explores performance in everyday life and aesthetic contexts through the use of performative writing. Using the alphabet as an organizational device, the book is composed of a series of short pieces that approach performance from multiple perspectives and rely upon various compositional strategies. It reaches toward the poetic, rhetorical, and relational in the desire to create dialogue. Some of the pieces are in keeping with a typical essay, others call upon literary forms and figures, others appear as personal narratives, and others come forward as quick speculations, experiments, or remarks. Together, they might best be read as rhizomatic thought trajectories where each piece "connects any point to any other point, and its traits are not necessarily linked to traits of the same nature" (Deleuze and Guattari, 1987, p. 21). The entries present complementary and oppositional logics, resisting a coherent theory of performance, although they are likely to point to the author's tendencies and biases.

The book moves playfully. It plays on the page in this performative act of writing about performance. While playing, it wants its language to remember its limits and its possibilities, to know how each word carries an ideological kick and how each word is marked by its representational failure, to sense how the body languages meaning and meaning languages the body, to turn back on itself to consider its own investments and their material consequences, and to evoke through sense and sensibility everyday and aesthetic performance. In short, the book acknowledges its location in the

Performance: An Alphabet of Performative Writing by Ronald J. Pelias, 7–22.

partial and partisan, strives for the evocative, reflexive, and embodied, and assumes material consequences.

The book might be read as a series of pieces designed as conversational starters. As such, they serve as beginning places, openings inviting dialogue. Or, the entries might be taken as performance nibbles, available as a snack whenever one wishes. The pieces can also be grouped together under central themes (see Appendix) to offer more extended commentary on a given subject. This may be helpful for those who wish to focus on a particular topic or to use the book as a complementary resource for class discussion. Despite the use of the alphabet, the book is not, however, an exhaustive dictionary or encyclopedia account. It includes subjects that are of interest to the author; it claims no more than that.

There are multiple audiences for this book; it is especially relevant, however, to those who are interested in theatre and performance studies. It approaches familiar topics often addressed by scholars in those fields, but it does so through the use of performative writing. Such a methodological move provides, I believe, a fresh slant on a number of well-known subjects. The book should also be of use to those who are interested in performative writing as a method. While the book takes as its subject performance, performative writing can be employed as a method for exploring any topic. The reader will see a variety of compositional strategies at play, strategies that provide a range of possibilities for using performative writing. The section below entitled "Performative Writing" (p. 11) is written to show in general how performative writing serves as a method for evoking human experiences. The section locates itself primarily in the work of scholars across the liberal and fine arts who embrace qualitative inquiry.

2
Going Places Together

Thank you for your generosity so far. I appreciate your willingness to pick up this book, to buy it, to take it home. And, how good of you to be reading, particularly given all the choices that you have. I appreciate your time and consideration. I know by now you've already made judgments. As we go on, you will have many more chances to decide whether you feel you are spending your time well. Even now, you may be thinking that this seems too contrived for your taste. As you know, you are always free to stop. I'll never know if you do. And if you are reading this because it was assigned for a class and you have decided that you've already had enough, here are a few things you can say that will give the impression that you read the whole book:

> "I like how the book gives all these different takes on performance."

> "Most of the pieces are too brief. I often feel the arguments would benefit from more sustained discussion."

> "The book positions me differently in regard to performance. It invites me to be both the person who does performance and the person who responds to it."

> "I agree that we must find alternative forms for writing about performance, forms that try to enter into the spirit of the subject. And these forms should do no harm to others as we go about our critical lives. Criticism, more than anything else, should be about the explanation and negotiation of feelings."

You may want to adapt these lines to fit in with the flow of the classroom conversation. After all, you probably don't want to argue for one of these claims if no one else is standing beside you.

As you probably know by now, this book uses the alphabet for its organizational structure. As you read the various entries, I hope there are times when you can stand with me in agreement. If you can't, I hope you will read against me, establishing a place where we might engage in dialogue. I must admit that I find I am not as comfortable as I would like with the stance of some of the pieces. I enjoy arguing against myself or being a devil's advocate. In general, though, the entries are about writing, about the aesthetic, about trying to get at what matters, about trying to get down why we are pulled to staged and everyday performances. As you read, I hope you feel that you are in art's presence or, at least, are persuaded that you should be.

If nothing more, I hope you would be willing to sample at least one or two pieces from the collection. You might consider going to the table of contents and seeing if any titles are tempting. If your primary interest is performance criticism, you might, for example, turn to "Appreciation" or "Insufficiency." If you like performing, you might, for instance, find "Becoming" or "Rehearsal" of interest. Or, if you love the performance of personal narratives as much as I do, you might, perhaps, want to look at "Confessions" or "Pledge." It doesn't matter in what order you might read the essays, and none should take you too long to get through—they are all easy reads. Or, if you like, just turn to "A" and begin. You are the judge every step of the way. It is, after all, your critical response that matters. While you are considering your options, I'll take a moment to thank those who have helped me put this book together.

I start with the wonderful colleagues in performance studies I've worked with at Southern Illinois University. I owe them considerable gratitude for their daily teachings about performance. To Lee Jenkins (San Francisco State University), Tami Spry (St. Cloud State University), and Tracy Stephenson Shaffer (Louisiana State University) I can only say that I keep each of you as a constant audience member in my head as I write. I owe considerable gratitude to Lesa Lockford (Bowling Green State University) and Nathan Stucky (Southern Illinois University) for their insightful conversations and work on the book. Mary Hinchcliff-Pelias (Southern Illinois University), my partner and first editor, allows me to rattle on about my projects and makes my writing much better than it would be without her keen critical eye. Mitch Allen and his staff at Left Coast Press continue to be the best team any author might hope to find. I also want to acknowledge the following publishers for their permission to reproduce in revised form the following essays: Sage, section 3 from "Beginnings" was published under the title, "Performative Writing as Scholarship: An Apology, An Argument, An Anecdote," *Cultural Studies↔Critical Methodologies* 5 (2005): 415–424; University California Press, entries entitled "Pledge" and "Opening" were published under the titles "Pledging Personal Allegiance to Qualitative Inquiry," *International Review of Qualitative Research* 2 (2009): 351–356, and "Performance Is an Opening," *International Review of Qualitative Research* 3 (2010): 173–174.

3
Performative Writing

In the desire to establish some definitional ground, I want to make six claims for performative writing, claims that point toward what I believe I am trying to do. First, performative writing expands the notions of what constitutes disciplinary knowledge. For some, that is just the problem. As Gingrich-Philbrook (1998) points out in his discussion of masculinity, fear of losing disciplinary control over sanctioned forms and content triggers a talk of legitimacy. Those who have been designated to legislate what counts had better stay ever vigilant, or the very foundation of the academic enterprise might crack, letting in all sorts of pollutants. This, it seems clear, is the sentiment behind Parks's (1998) fearful claim, "No question is more central to our identity as scholars than the question of what counts as scholarship" (np). Parks's fear cannot be easily dismissed, but in the case of performative writing, it is misplaced.

Performative writing is not the wrecking ball swinging into the academic house. While most would acknowledge that scholarship is contingent upon historical, economic, ideological, and disciplinary patterns, few are ready to reject the considerable body of scholarly work in the name of relativism. Every time a paper is graded, an article for a journal is reviewed, or a scholarly essay is written, scholars are reflecting and affirming what they value. To argue contingency is not to argue for the utterly arbitrary: There are some good reasons for valuing what scholars have. In this sense, one might agree with Parks. Parks, however, need not fear performative writing. It is at most a hairline fracture in the academic foundation, a fracture that has been noticeable for years as scholars have attempted to force the scientific paradigm to answer their questions. Despite the fact that many have declared the logical positivist house in ruins, scholars continue to reside there. Despite the fact that many have shown how building structures with the mind only is flawed architecture, scholars continue to do so. The performative writing fracture may help academic houses settle into greater alignment with human experience. Performative writing fixes the fracture by adding design features; it welcomes the body into the mind's dwellings.

It is also useful to remember that formal argument based in and upon the methods of scientific inquiry is not the mode for discovering truths; it is, like all modes of inquiry, nothing more than a rhetorical style. Scholars need not be tied to the belief or practice that their scholarship must look a particular way, particularly a paradigmatic way that has its uses but has limited power in accounting for human experience. Instead, scholars might embrace another rhetorical style, what Goodall (1991) calls "mystery," "to encourage us to see and to define situations by their unique human and spiritual poetic, the interpenetrations of self, Other, and context, by our complexity and interdependence rather than by some simpler linear or causal logic" (p. 125).

Second, performative writing features lived experience, telling, iconic moments that call forth the complexities of human life. With lived experience, there is no separation between mind and body, objective and subjective, cognitive and affective. Human experience does not reduce to numbers, to arguments, to abstractions. As poet Stephen Dunn (1994) notes, "Oh abstractions are just abstract // until they have an ache in them" (p. 212). Performative writing attempts to keep the complexities of human experience intact, to place the ache back in scholars' abstractions.

This is not to argue that experience equals scholarship. Performative writing does not indiscriminately record experience; it does not simply duplicate a cinema verite experiment. Instead, performative writing is a highly selective camera, aimed carefully to capture the most arresting angles. Each frame is studied and felt; each shot is significant. Much is left on the editing floor. Everyday experience, then, is not scholarship, but the shaping of everyday experience into telling and moving tales can be. The performative writer functions as States (1996) suggests the artist does, as "someone who says, 'This is the way people behave *N* number of times,' and knows how to put the *N* into expressive form" (p. 19).

In this manner, performative writing makes its case, a case, to borrow from Fisher's (1987) familiar argument, based in narrative plausibility and narrative fidelity. It is a case that is more interested in evoking than representing, in constructing a world than in positing this is the way the world is (for example, Tyler, 1986; Ellis, 1995).

It is a case that does not just rely upon its descriptive portrayal, no matter how precise or poignant, but also depends upon its ability to create experience. Tyler's (1986) assertion about post-modern ethnography holds for performative writing as well: "It is not a record of experience at all; it is the means of experience" (p. 138). Thus, performative writing offers both an evocation of human experience and an enabling fiction. Its power is in its ability to tell the story of human experience, a story that can be trusted and a story that can be used. It opens the doors to a place where the raw and the genuine find their articulation through form, through poetic expression, through art.

Third, performative writing rests upon the belief that the world is not given, but constructed, composed of multiple realities. All representations of human experience are partial and partisan (for example, Goodall, 1989, 1991, 1996, 2000; Phelan, 1993, 1997). At best, scholars might achieve, to use Clifford's (1986) phrase, a "rigorous partiality" (p. 25) and acknowledge, like all "standpoint epistemologists,"[1] that all our utterances are committed, positioned. Performative writing resists arguments that attempt to prove all other explanations inadequate or suspect. Performative writers do not believe that the world is one particular way. They do not believe that argument is an opportunity to win, to impose their logic upon others, to colonize. They do not believe that there should be only one house on the hill. They do not believe that they can speak without speaking themselves, without carrying their own vested interests, their own personal histories, their own philosophical and theoretical assumptions forward. They do not believe that they can write without loss, without mourning (Phelan, 1997), without metonymy (Pollock, 1998).

Performative writing, then, takes as its goal to dwell within multiple perspectives, to celebrate an interplay of voices, to privilege dialogue over monologue. It cherishes the fragmentary, the uncertain. It marks the place that poet Tess Gallagher wishes to locate, the "point of all possibilities" where "time collapses, drawing in the past, present and future" (1982, p. 107).

Four, performative writing often evokes identification and empathic responses. It creates a space where others might see themselves. Although written in a variety of forms, it often presents what

Trinh Minh-ha (1991) calls a "plural I," an "I" that has the potential to stand in for many "I's." It is an "I" that resonates, that resounds, that is familiar. Performative writing also often beckons empathy, allowing others to not only see what the writer might see but also to feel what the writer might feel. It is an invitation to take another's perspective.

Through identification and empathy, then, readers become implicated and human experience concretized. Readers see more clearly how they and others constitute and are constituted by the world. They come to feel that they and others are written, given voice, a voice that they did not have prior to the reading. In this sense, the "I" of performative writing might best be seen as a geographical marker, a "here" rather than a "self." In short, the self becomes a positional possibility (Garber, 1995).

When performative writing does not point beyond the writer, it may appear self-indulgent, narcissistic, self-serving or, to put it perhaps more kindly, therapeutic. This was one of the many attacks upon the *Text and Performance Quarterly (*1997) special issue on performative writing.[2] The argument was simple: If an article had such qualities, surely it wasn't of any value. No one, however, seemed to question why one might object to the self being indulged, reflexive, served, or healed within scholarly work. On occasion, some noted the history of legitimating practices as if that were proof enough (that is, it hasn't been allowed; therefore, it shouldn't be allowed) (for example, Wendt, 1998).

Yet, notions of self-indulgence, narcissism, self-serving, and therapeutic do seem to disturb, to rub against what scholars hope their research might achieve. For such scholarship is not just about the self, although the self can never be left behind. Such scholarship, even when based upon the self, points outward. Its aim is to tell about human experience. It is for this reason that identification, that space of recognition and resonance, is often an essential aspect of performative writing. Moreover, the self can be a place where tensions are felt and uncovered, a place of discovery, a place of power, of political action and resistance. One often knows what matters by recognizing what the body feels. This is in part the lesson phenomenologists have been trying to teach for years (for example, Leder, 1990; Sheets-Johnstone, 1990).

Five, performative writing turns the personal into the political and the political into the personal. It starts with the recognition that individual bodies provide a potent data base for understanding the political and that hegemonic systems write upon individual bodies. This is, of course, only to articulate what feminists have understood for years: the personal is political. It is to realize the potential in Benjamin's (1979) insight, "To live in a glass house is a revolutionary virtue par excellence. It is also an intoxication, a moral exhibitionism, that we badly need" (p. 228). Yet, too often research, even feminist and Marxist, does not call into play its own insights; it does not call upon individual experience to make its case. It does not work behind closed doors. It does not show how politics matter to individual lives or how individual lives are evidence that social justice is absent. Performative writing insists upon making such connections. It is, to use Pollock's (1998) word, "consequential." It offers, as Denzin (2003) puts it, "kernels of utopian hope, suggestions for how things might be different, and better" (p. xi).

Six, performative writing participates in relational and scholarly contexts. No writing occurs without context. In traditional work, the burden is to demonstrate how a particular argument advances current knowledge, a movement toward some all-encompassing explanation. The relationship between the writer and the reader is a distanced one, a relational positioning that demands that neither person become connected to the other. Performative writing, on the other hand, assumes that at given times certain questions are of interest, not because their answers might be another step toward some final explanation, but because of how they connect people within a scholarly community and locate them as individuals.

Some questions are productive to embrace because they participate in the ongoing concerns of a scholarly community. Performative writing, when done well, understands its place within disciplinary history. As it participates in that tradition, sometimes explicitly and sometimes implicitly, it hopes to provide "thick descriptions" (Geertz, 1983), "experiential particularity" (Baumeister and Newman, 1994), "deconstructive verisimilitude" (Denzin, 1997), "theatrical narrativity" (Crapanzano, 1986). Any piece of performative writing is a story among many but a story about issues that matter or can be made to matter to the community.

Some questions are productive to embrace because they connect individuals, not just as scholars, but as people who are willing to place themselves at personal risk. By confessing, by exposing, and by witnessing, performative writers pursue their scholarly interests. In doing so, what might have remained hidden is made public, what might have stayed buried is put under examination, what might have been kept as personal commitment becomes public testimony. Such efforts often ask readers to respond, not just at the level of idea, but as one person who has become connected to another. Performative writers offer readers an interpersonal contract that they can elect to engage.

This section finds its fitting end with the words of poet Philip Booth: "I strongly feel that every poem, every work of art, everything that is well done, well made, well said, genuinely given, adds to our chances of survival by making the world and our lives more habitable" (1989, p. 37). Performative writing participates in this spirit, in the hope that current research might become a place where all are welcome to reside and where all might come to recognize themselves in all their human complexity.

4
A Gathering

Consider (1) what is on the table, (2) how it has all been placed before you, and (3) why it is there for you to consume. First, around the table are my colleagues. They are looking, seeing how I've served them up for your pleasure. Some are central influences who I write and write, hoping that I might somehow get down how their work has shaped my thinking. Around the table, too, are my students whom I've tried to serve well. More often than not, though, I've left our encounters feeling I should have done a better job. Finally, there are those I know only by some act of momentary audiencing. I've always enjoyed looking. I apologize to them all for using them to serve my interests.

In the middle of it all, I am there as a stuffed bird, the centerpiece, the dominant taste, eager for all to build a meal around me. I lie before you having had a long and full career. I'm glad to give myself up for this moment together. Given my central place on the table, I cannot be ignored. Cooked, I cannot fly away, even if that were my wish. I hope you like fowl. Please add your own sauce. As you might guess, my preference would be for a light one. But truly, my desire is not to be the main course.

Also coming to the table are performances, a variety of seasonings and textures that turn the ordinary into art and art into the ordinary. Each requires a clean palate if you are to be fully satisfied. Knowing when manners are followed and when they are broken helps but isn't essential. I hope that you can savor the taste of each spice and that I have added enough of them bring out the flavor.

In the mix of it all is an argument, passed around from hand to hand, put in one mouth after another. For some, the argument is over-done, burnt; it was left in the oven for too long without a cook's careful eye. It is spit out. For others, the argument melts in the mouth; it's a sweet for all that has turned sour. Notice how savory it is.

Finally, there is a bit of wine which could just as easily be taken for a tear or a drop of blood. It spoils the linen but reminds you that you have eaten.

I apologize if what I served isn't enough for you or if it isn't sensitive to your dietary needs. I tried to offer both the cooked and the raw. I admit I'm suspicious of people who like everything that's put in front of them, but I do hope there is something here for you, something that you can swallow. If not, there is no need to throw out what others might enjoy. After all, out there are academics in need of nourishment.

The book is here for you to consume. Take small bites if you prefer, sampling here and there. No one will find everything to his or her liking. I won't try to force feed you. Whether to eat or not is always your choice. But perhaps, having had a little encouragement, you have discovered or will find something that you truly enjoy. More and more people are welcoming this kind of cuisine into their diets. They say once you acquire a taste for it, it's hard to stop indulging yourself. They say it seems more natural. They say it makes them healthier.

After you are finished, excuse yourself from the table. I'm sure you are tired of being told how to savor the smells, how to chew on this and that, and how to swallow it all down. First, feel free to take whatever you like. If you've found anything to your taste, please take it with you. Second, know that I'm open for suggestions. You can send any thoughts to rpelias@siu.edu. Perhaps we can chat. There is always more to learn in the kitchen.

5
Performance

Performance:

1. An act, a doing, behavior
2. An art, an aesthetic form

6
A Critical Stance

He thinks he knows what he likes and what he doesn't.

He likes when he is vulnerable, open, not because he is an exhibitionist or because he thinks his views are so interesting or different from others, but because he believes that by fully sharing his perspectives he might make a human connection, he might uncover what matters in performance, and he might feel honest. He worries how he might be read, but recognizes that no one ever has control over such matters. He worries that he cannot take anything back, but knows that everything he says is only a part of an ongoing conversation. He likes that what he shared is what he felt.

He dislikes when his research hides behind the illusion of objectivity, when his research reduces complexity into significance claims, when his research asserts Truth. Surely he should know by now that the body will never equal a number, that the body will never settle into a proposition, that the body will never reduce to a problem to be solved. The body, in order to live, must have a heart.

He likes when his language tries to enter that heart. Then, his words allow him to get some sense of the center, the beginning point, the raw. Motive often finds its way to metaphor. When he is getting at the feel of things, he feels he is doing what he should. He likes to lean in.

He dislikes when his language is direct, flat as an instruction manual. It is never about how to put everything together. Without searching underneath the directions, he cannot even see what is there. Without the curves and claws, without the spills and slips, without the rough and the rhythmic, his words are nothing more than a repetitive grammar, an empty nest, a broken lever.

He likes that he has spent many years thinking about performance. Its impact on his life, he believes, cannot be overstated. He thinks he is more sensitive to its power, to its ability to inflate and deflate, to its efforts to position people by the products they produce. After seeing its offerings, he is pleased that he was not silenced, that he sought a new discourse, a discourse that attempts to speak through art.

He dislikes that sometimes he forgets what he has learned. Too often his critical remarks are nothing more than his attempt to put on display what he thinks he knows. Too often his critical responses forget the person for whom his responses might matter in the name of some idea or some principle when, in actuality, the only idea or principle worth remembering is that all criticism comes to rest on someone's body. Too often his judgments spring forth as pronouncements from a Mount Olympus of his own imagination. He should know that there is no speaking as a god.

He likes that he completed the manuscript, one sentence at a time. The long hours hunched over his computer fade. The moments of frustration when he couldn't find the right words fall away. The times he lost faith slip by. He sees himself holding the finished product in his hands for the first time and he smiles. He has always loved books.

He dislikes how the book might be treated by the critics he was hoping to persuade. He sees it tossed aside, unread. He sees it marked with angry comments in the margins. He sees it reviewed with professional courtesy but with disdain. He is sad.

7

Mind/Body

Never let the mind or the body become the other's synecdoche. Be a hammer to my bent nail, a saw to my broken branch, a chisel to my bland finish. Come close. Be right here.

8
A Final Thought Before We Continue

I need to say something to you now. Don't be alarmed. I don't think what I have to say will surprise or disturb you, and if you don't want to accept what I will offer, that's fine. No negative consequences will follow. But, if you hope to have the relationship that I think we both want, then I need certain things from you. Quite honestly, if these are things you can't give, then we should part ways. I won't be angry with you or resent your choice. I know there are multiple demands on your time beyond what we share together. For my part, as I proceed, I will try my best to keep your interest. I believe that is something you want. And as I try to keep your interest, I'm hoping you will focus on what I have to say. Let's make this just between us. We can't get very far if we don't start here.

As we move on, please attend not only to what I am saying, but also to how I am saying it. I can't begin to tell you the number of hours I've spent finding what I want to say and how I want to say it. I've thought about what I should say when, about the arguments I'm trying to make, and about how I want you to feel when I'm finished. I've considered your possible resistance. For me, the how is just as important as the what—they really can't be separated. Any writer will tell you that. Just think about the countless love stories you've encountered. They are always about two people trying to find their way to each other. It's the how that makes us want to hear another love story, that separates the good ones from the boring ones. As I go on, I'll do my best not to bore you, and I'll do that by thinking long and hard about how I say what I want to say. In return, I need you to appreciate word choices that give the familiar a productive kick; sentences that move you along with ease, turning this way and that, capturing the complexities of the ins and outs, discovering nuances through details, or that come as quick as a telling glimpse; and arguments, by carrying much more than logical proof, show why a given point matters, why it has consequences in human lives, why affect can't be left out of any human account. I won't always succeed in giving you such things, but I will always try, and I would truly appreciate it if you would occasionally pause to consider if such things are there.

I might just mention here an important associated point. Please hear me out before you claim you know me or dismiss what I'm offering. If you decide you don't want a relationship after a few moments, that's fine. You can just leave. I'll be disappointed, but I'd rather you walk away early on than pretend that you are interested in what I have to say without hearing me out. And please, don't quote me if you are just going to tune in now and then. Although I may be wrong, everything I say I believe is worth saying; otherwise, I wouldn't be saying it. I'm sure you've had the experience of someone telling you what you think or assuming she or he understands you before you have a chance to explain yourself. It's frustrating, isn't it? Often it just feels rude, doesn't it? Please, don't be that person. You'll know when my turn is done. I'll welcome your response after I'm finished.

In anticipation of your response, I want to remind you that I'm doing the best I know how. I hope you appreciate that, and I hope that you will be generous. I'm hoping that as we move along, you'll be able to think about what might be of use to you instead of what's wrong with what I've said. We spend too much of our time letting our critical teeth tear into the work of others. It feels rather violent, don't you think? It seldom makes for good relationships. I'm surely not trying to say that you can't disagree with me, but there is no reason for either of us to make our case at the expense of the other or to form some alliance against others who don't happen to see or do things the way we do. When you disagree with me or become disappointed in something I've said or how I've said it, please feel free to say so, but let's not play a game of "got you now." We should be in this together, working always to put our best feet forward. Sometimes we might step together; other times we won't. In either case, we can best find our stride if we go forward with respect and care.

Respect, you might say, is earned, and there are things that you see me doing that you just can't abide. I can accept that. My way of proceeding sometimes breaks away from expected models for doing things. I know that. But I hope you think there is some value in testing limits. I don't much like playing the role of academic police, and I would guess that you don't either. Let's leave our police in the closet whenever we can. We will be better people if we do, people that others might want around.

As I said before, it helps when we have a shared commitment. I want your considered thoughts, so that we can be better together. I'll try not to make you angry with me, but I need to know when I do. I'll try to be sensitive to you, but I need to know when I am not. I'll try not to disgust you, but I need to know if I'm making you turn away. On a more positive note, I'll love it if you tell me what I've said moves or intrigues you, if it is of some emotional use to you. I'll love knowing if you entered the emotional space I was trying to create. I know this is asking quite a bit of you. I do need you to be receptive, open, vulnerable, reflexive. When we are connecting heart to heart, I feel we are where we belong. Isn't this what we really want?

So, please, give me something in return. I can deal with almost anything, but silence is by far the hardest. In relational terms, the silent treatment is called stonewalling. Building a stone wall between us won't get us very far. I realize that you are free, encouraged often, to do whatever you wish with utterances that come your way. You are entitled to do so. It's the postmodern go-to position, and there are some good reasons for going down that road. But that keeps us from creating something together, keeps us from connecting with one another, keeps us apart. I'd rather move forward by being present to you, by trying to make us work. I believe acting in this way, bringing an attentive sensitivity to our time together, will place us in the most productive and most caring relationship to one another. I hope you can go there with me.

Notes

1. For an excellent discussion of "standpoint epistemologies" see Denzin (1997). In the chapter entitled "Standpoint Epistemologies," he examines the assumptions of standpoint texts by focusing on the work of Patrica Hill Collins, Trinh T. Minh-ha, and Gloria Anzaldua.
2. The infamous *Text and Performance Quarterly* special issue (January 1997) produced a flurry of CRTNET NEWS postings, convention programs, and published responses.

Appreciation

For an appreciative, compassionate criticism:

Applaud

Announce your pleasure, even if minor, even if your disappointments seem to be pushing forward, even if you want nothing more than to escape. Clap as loud as a duck quacking for the bread spread out on the ground. Pound your hands together until you hammer in what deserves applause. Make sure you've been heard.

Beckon

Call forward the heart of the matter. Be pleased when you know it is near. Feel it beat in your hands. Hold it firmly until it pulses through your body like a drug. Become addicted, at least for a moment in time.

Confess

Tell what you would rather not. Tell about yourself. Tell how it entered you, how ready you were for it to come, how it has changed you. Remember, your critical comments always say more about you than the object of your commentary. Banish any fear.

Dwell

Inhabit it until it is as comfortable as a pair of your old shoes, as recognizable as your own signature, as familiar as your own dwelling. Drop into it, settle, and relax. Come to believe you are with an old friend.

Performance: An Alphabet of Performative Writing by Ronald J. Pelias, 23–27.

Emulate

Learn its voice, its rhythm, its dreams. Live with it. Live in it. Wear it like a tailored suit, like a glove, like a second skin. Become its impostor, speaking from inside it as if you have always belonged there. Watch it become you. Then, return it to its rightful owner.

Finger

Run through it with the skills of an old librarian who moves through a card catalogue to see what is there. Learn its "a" to "z." Find the drawers of its references. Bend to read the information you need. Caress the cards that matter.

Graze

Feed on it, content as a cow in a field of green. Invite others—some who are like you and some who are not—into your pasture. Chew on it, working it over and over until it is ready to digest. Ruminate. Then, start again.

Hasten

Lose no time. Remember, a life is at stake. Take responsibility for the actions that might be needed. Act quickly. When necessary, your job is to free the arteries, to do bypass surgery, and to massage the heart. Use electric shock only as a last resort.

Ignite

With enough effort, everything can be made to burn. Work your words until they are kindling. Find what is just smoldering and fan it. There can never be enough oxygen. Know how fire consumes, how it seduces, how it calls. Enjoy the combustion. Douse nothing.

Jump

Like a young boy who hangs frozen for the first time suspended from a rope over a deep water hole, know that you must let go. Remember that the moment before you drop is always the most frightening. Release your grip and plummet down. Know that the pleasures of plunging deep below the surface are what will convince you to jump in again.

Kiss

Following the extended glances, the flirtations, and the soft promises, bring it into your arms. Hold it firmly, looking into its eyes and feeling its skin. Sense its warmth against your body. Wonder why on this particular day a new lover has come into your life. Kiss in the bewilderment of it all.

Labor

Work your body until it sweats, its muscles loosen, and it can take all pain in stride. Work your mind until it can't be stopped, until it is electrified by possibilities and terrorized by failure. Your goal is to give birth.

Massage

Rub each word with adjectives, penetrating as deep as syntax, sliding as smoothly as the sentence, and coming down as hard as an exclamation point. Moisten its skin. As skin comes to skin, connect. Don't stop until your palms find the spine.

Nail

Even though something always will remain loose, nail down whatever you can. It will give you a house where you can reside. Decide if you want to buy it. See what improvements might be needed. Check for leaking faucets, cracks in the walls, and damaged floorboards. If you must, replace the roof with a new name.

Observe

Magnify. Bring it into focus. Place it under a microscope so that each detail will be apparent, so that its intricate life, its permeable cells, its genetic structure will unfold before your eyes. Then, stand back. Look at it through a telescope and watch its universe expand. Remember, everything, including yourself, wobbles.

Pardon

Know that it will only flourish if not locked up. Your job is not to police. Instead, be a compassionate judge. Excuse. Do what is best for all involved. Seldom does it make sense to remove someone from the family. No one should be put away and forgotten.

Query

Question only your motives. Wonder why you want to know what you do. Consider why you are pointing where you are. Examine how often you say the things you do. Ponder whether now is the right time and place to say what you feel you must. Contemplate how you say what you do. Reflect upon whom your comments are really about.

Release

Let yourself go. React. It is permissible to respond, to shed a tear, to become angry. Reassure yourself that by doing so you are only being human. Remember, being human is a fine way to be. Remember all the wonderful people you have known who have been that way.

Search

Assume you are on a quest for treasure. Cut through whatever forest you must pass; climb whatever mountain that stands in your way; navigate whatever body of water you must cross. Believe that all your efforts will lead to your reward. In the end, when you have done everything that you possibly could, discover that the quest was the treasure.

Trade

Everyone has goods. Give your beads for its bracelet, your bread for its wine, your sweat for its calluses. In the market of ideas, see what is there. Know the value of what you have to offer. Do not overestimate. The profit is in the exchange. Beware of only browsing. Swap your heart for its lungs.

Unearth

See what is buried beneath the bones. Feel for a faint pulse. See the life there. See it struggling to get out of its deep cave. See where it wants to go. See how to help it crawl from its bed, how to brush the dirt from its clothes, how to welcome it back. See why it is wanted. See who it is.

Vow

To the Muses, to Apollo, and to Dionysus pledge your allegiance. Swear upon all that is written that you will never use words to harm, to rip the heart from those who might be struggling to live, to work yourself into the center of attention. Swear this and more on the grave of those who brought you here. Make an oath. Promise everything.

Wrestle

Fight it to the ground. Let your body twist and turn around it as you try to pin it down. Watch it slip away. Know that you are in a struggle. Hope only for a draw. Realize that there will never be a three count—a one, two, three that ends it all.

X-out

Cross out nothing. That's not your job. Point here and there to places that seem to offer the fewest rewards. Know that in the pointing you are pointing to yourself. Know that the "x" blots out, obliterates, destroys. Know that the "x" yells "no."

Yearn

After you think you are done, cry for another chance. Return to the place of the offering and search for what you missed. See if you can meet again so that you can say what you need to say now. Remember, reaching out lives in the hope of a future. Crave what's next.

Zero

When everything is working, the sum of one plus one is one. One minus one is an empty whole. The sum of all that is said and done is what you can circle.

B

Becoming

A decision
to reach,
to listen,
to lean in,
a turned head, an earnest ear, a set eye,
ready,
ready to stretch,
to slide closer,
closer,
a search for what might be there,
filled with assumptions, habits,
ways of doing,
but guarding against the easy take,
anticipating,
relishing the familiar
and the strange,
wanting to find
the person in and between words,
the heart, located in desire,
the body, built with attitude
the reasons, found in the logic of why.

Performance: An Alphabet of Performative Writing by Ronald J. Pelias, 29–31.

An entry,
a taking on, part by part, a trying on, bit by bit,
rejecting and accepting, choosing,
breathing into the yes and the maybe,
the turn of the hand, the sound of the
named, the feel of the claimed,
pushing aside the no,
a vine wrapping itself around,
wanting to know which way to turn, which
way to attach,
questioning, maneuvering, considering,
playing, imagining, wondering
if one might cling to another
without damage, without danger,
without dissent.

A knowing,
a performative claim   an argument   a case
based in hard deliberation   attention   reflection
following a decision tree: grounded,   branches to
branches
stems to stems   leaves to leaves
until the parched is satisfied,
an embodied act   felt   visceral
based in the telling body   the sensuous   the somatic
the heart's method: feeling the pulse, breathing each
breath,
waist deep
until the head knows its heart and the heart knows its head.

A holding,
a firm knot, a keeping, an earned comfort,
sensing it as your own, inhabiting, making it a home,
settling in, finding comfort, a familiarity, a fabric,
feeling secure, knowing what is locked in and locked out
a set script, stylized, learned with repetition, found, figured,
a recognized habit, moving into the bones,
a worn path, remembered through sweat,
a deep cut, worked slowly into the skin.

A becoming,
the self turned, transformed, tagged as another, possessing
what can never be possessed, tailored to a shape, touched,
transported, standing in thanks and regrets, knowing what
is loss, what is gained, knowing only the translated trace,
knowing the triumphant and troubling trespass, knowing
the theology of the intertwined.

Concealment

The story I tell of how my first marriage ended always includes the same details: After seven years of marriage, after surviving the year I was in Vietnam, and after the birth of our son, it was over in a flash. One day we decided to take in a film—Barbra Streisand and Robert Redford in "The Way We Were." We were sitting in the theater waiting for the film to start when Ann started crying. "What's the matter?" I asked. Through her sobs, she answered: "I'm leaving you. Tom and I are in love." Tom happened to be my best friend at the time. The next day Ann and my son were gone. I was in shock—I thought our marriage was on solid ground. At this point I typically add a quick footnote to lighten the moment: We didn't stay to see the film.

This story, in slightly altered form, is one I've used in my writing. It carries a degree of disclosiveness that is often found with performances of personal narratives and autoethnographic research. In this piece, I want to turn on my own writing to examine what is gained and lost by sharing what is often kept private. I examine how the "self" is often constructed in a positive light, even when revealing its most negative aspects, and how that positive construction of self, although perhaps deceptive, may function productively. In other words, I wish to look at some of the issues that surround revealing the often concealed in our performance and scholarly work.

Performance: An Alphabet of Performative Writing by Ronald J. Pelias, 33–51.

Revealing the Often Concealed

I have been persuaded by the interpersonal, artistic, and social activist argument that revealing the private self to others carries productive power. In the early 1970s, a time when I was deeply influenced by third force psychologists Karl R. Rogers, William C. Schutz, and Abraham H. Maslow and when I was leading encounter groups every weekend in my home, I stumbled across a little book entitled, *Why Am I Afraid to Tell You Who I Am?* by John Powell (1969). Targeted to a general public, Powell's book suggests that our fear is located in the belief that "if I tell you who I am, you may not like who I am, and it is all that I have" (p. 27). He answers that concern by asking if we want to be liked for someone who we are not. This simple logic I found seductive and saw it repeated in various forms in the interpersonal communication literature of day. But it isn't just a reflection of those touchy-feely times; such arguments continue in interpersonal texts. For example, Johnson (2009) writes, "Healthy relationships are built on self-disclosure....If you cannot reveal yourself, you cannot become close to others, and you cannot be valued by others" (pp. 255–56). Canary, Cody, and Manusov (2002) offer a similar claim: "It [self-disclosure] is the most controllable method you have of indicating to others just who you are" (p. 198).

In a similar vein, many creative writers have felt the pull of the disclosive. The influence of the Beats and the Confessional poets still finds its articulation in contemporary poetry. Autobiography and memoir heavily mark the current literary scene. And it is not uncommon to find writers noting how personal biography, even in the most fictional work, informs their efforts. Lamontt (1994), for example, notes:

> We write to expose the unexposed. If there is one door in the castle you have been told not to go through, you must. Otherwise, you'll just be rearranging furniture in rooms you've already been in. Most human beings are dedicated to keeping that one door shut. But the writer's job is to see what's behind it, to see the bleak unspeakable stuff, and to turn the unspeakable into words. (p. 198)

Looking behind shut doors is not just a strategy for discovering one's personal voice, for stirring the imagination, or for writing a truthful self. It also reveals the hegemonic power that is at play.

Writing beyond the permissible is to write into existence what has been silenced. Its power resides in the resonance it creates in its readers. That is why the "personal is political." As hooks (1999) notes,

> I am most interested in confessional writing when it allows us to move into the personal as a way to go beyond it. In all my work I evoke the personal as a prelude. It functions as a welcoming gesture, offering the reader a sense of who I am, a sense of location. (p. 67)

Establishing a sense of location creates a rallying point for social activist work; it calls forward those who've been told that their experiences do not matter or do not exist.

This quick and familiar review of the personal, literary, and political benefits of revealing the concealed could stand as a justification for opening this essay with the story about the end of my first marriage. On a personal level, sharing my relational history allows me to stand as an open self and permits others, if they so desire, entry into my life, into some understanding of my vulnerabilities and perhaps my behaviors. More generally, it participates as narrative data for those interested in relational termination. It tells us something about the human condition. From a literary perspective, the story carries a dramatic punch and has a few ironic touches but, more importantly, taps into a relational experience, whether lived or imagined, that may resonate. It has the makings for a good story. Shock, betrayal, and emotional pain crawl around those sentences, offering the reader a glance at an experience no one would welcome. And to the extent that it finds resonance, it becomes political, calling into question the institution of marriage, its privileges and hegemonic weight. Yet, despite what the story reveals, it also conceals.

Concealment in the Revealed

Dunn (1994) writes, "I love that there's a secret / behind every secret I ever told" (p. 279). I, too, find pleasure in the secrets behind the secrets I've told. My pleasure in telling my relational termination story arises, in part, from how I've managed to construct myself. I am the victim, the person wronged, betrayed. Usually when I tell this tale, I get a sympathetic response which allows me to then say something like, "We were both young. Just stupid kids. Really too young to marry." In such an utterance, I become understanding, forgiving, perhaps even gracious. What I do not do, what secrets behind the secret I do not share, is tell the tale in a manner that positions me poorly. I do not tell the story from her point of view. I do not tell how during that time I was putting most of my efforts into my first academic job, paying little attention to her, and expecting her to happily fulfill the traditional role of wife and mother. I do not tell that my introduction to feminist thought was still several years ahead of me. I do not tell that during my tour of duty in Vietnam, I was fifth in line for a Vietnamese woman who did not speak or move during the entire time of our encounter. I do not tell that I let my son go.

"Paradoxical as it sounds," Lopate (1996) writes,

> American poetry today suffers not from being too personal and confessional, but from being not personal and confessional enough. Often the poet pulls back from providing just those biographical specificities and idiosyncratic reactions that would bring him alive as an authentic individual. (p. 39)

Such is the case with my tale. It buries the secrets behind the secret and, in so doing, reduces its complexity as it masquerades as an authentic self. It is both factually true—everything I said did happen—and it is a lie.

Gunn (2006) might say, as he has before (pp. 91–92), that my tale is just another example of "perfumativity," discourse tamed by a hygienic apparatus, cornered by a relentless surveillance eye and always after an order and control that suggests one's shit doesn't stink. But, of course, it does, and, as Gunn notes, there is power in producing "our gifts freely and with selfless abandon" (p. 93). Only then can we escape our own constipation.

Poetic constipation is Hoagland's (2003) concern:

> Much of our mainstream poetry is confined by an ethic of sincerity and the unstated wish to be admired (if not admired, liked; if not liked, sympathized with). American poetry still largely believes, as romantics have for a few hundred years, that a poem is straightforward autobiographical testimony to, among other things, the decency of the speaker. (p. 13)

Like Gunn, Hoagland finds "the problem with such civility is that it excludes all kinds of subject matter which cannot be handled without contamination of the handler" (p. 13). He calls for writing from the often unforgivable and prohibited place of "meanness," a place where truth-telling can be found.

"Overproduc[ing] our shit" as an act of resistance (Gunn, p. 94) or becoming uninhibitedly mean as a strategy for speaking truth (Hoagland) is not an easy task for most people. Hoagland is right—people want to be admired, liked, sympathized with. That is why we all have our face-saving, or should I say to be more accurate, face-serving, narratives. The stories we tell position us, for better or worse, and mindful tellers are always keenly aware that their literary choices carry rhetorical consequences. We construct selves, for ourselves and others, that we can live with and that make us into people we would like to be. In doing so, details are lost, biases are present, and hegemonic structures at times are held in place. In this sense, we are all guilty of the narratives we tell—they are, more often than not, ideologically suspect half-truths.

The Productivity of Revealing and Concealing

Knowing that there is always more to reveal is, as we all recognize, representation's nemesis. We have designed multiple strategies (for example, Madison's [2005] possibilizing, Pollock's [1998] nervousness) to address this issue, allowing us to dance lightly on anything that might appear as firm ground. We rightly carry some skepticism in the face of totalizing narratives. We mark our claims with quotations, put question marks after the declarative, and cross out the given. Such maneuvering allows us to acknowledge the partisan and the partial. But choosing not to reveal what we know might be revelatory because it positions us poorly is another matter. Such a move is a falsification that diminishes complexity, purifies motives, and constructs dubious saints. It keeps us from presenting ourselves as we understand ourselves to be, from offering an authentic presence, and from embracing our own humanness. Such a move, however, may also write us into the people we wish to become.

When I finished writing *A Methodology of the Heart* (2004), Mitch Allen, then editor of the AltaMira series, described the book to me in an appealingly dismissive way. He said, "It's just a book about a big old guy being sensitive." I was aware of trying to write a sensitive self and I feel the burden of living up to that construction. When I tell my first marriage story, I don't want to be the person who treated my wife in a manner that justifies her actions. By not sharing such evidence, I create a speaker closer to the person I want to be, a person who I can come to believe I am, particularly if others treat me in keeping with that construction. I can become the person I created. I can become a better self. In other circumstances, if I were to write about how my behavior led to uncorrectable sorrow or unspeakable wrongs, I can only do so by asking for forgiveness. Otherwise, I become the person who is comfortable causing uncorrectable sorrow or unspeakable wrongs. I must be ethically present, both in acknowledging past errors and calling for future actions. I must be accountable and trust that change is possible.

What I reveal and conceal are strategies for being, ethically charged, located in past and future actions, and consequential for myself and others. My stories, with all their secrets, both hidden and revealed, constitute me. I am always a being becoming, whose narrative trails are evidence of negotiated authenticity, intractable facts, and ethical promises.

Confessions

Performance 1: The assignment was simple: Tell a story from your family history. Most of the stories the students selected to tell were comic in nature—the family trip when everything went wrong, the aunt who blurted out everything that came to mind, the silly fight between a brother and a sister. Sheryl Thomas (fictive name) chose a different tack. She told the tale of losing her mother to cancer when she was eight years old and how her dad died just two years later in a car accident. The story focused on the number of times she would find herself in situations where people would assume she had two living parents. She talked about how that assumption often struck her as insensitive, even cruel. The performance was not maudlin or self-pitying but presented with such a light touch and precise details that it was particularly powerful. When she finished, the class, deeply moved, offered enthusiastic and sustained applause.

After the applause was dying down and Sheryl was settling into her seat, she said, changing the mood of the moment, "I just love telling death stories. You can get the audience every time." The audience seemed stunned, not quite sure what to make of Sheryl's comment. Sensing the audience was puzzled, Sheryl exclaimed, "Oh, none of that was true. I made it all up. I just thought it would make a good story." And she was right; it had.

Performance 2: Jen Tuder invited the audience to a meal at her "House of Narrative." She ushered us to a candle-lit, banquet table where she gave us a menu which read:

Entrees

S/M Jen—Sinfully rich, this entree features taboo sexually nestled in a bed of politics.

Burying My Father—A complex dish with the dark, robust flavors of suicide, family secrets, and redemption served with a side of righteous indignation.

Desserts

Forgetting & Remembering—Theory abounds in this

> selection, imported fresh from literary criticism.
> Advice is smoothly blended with the light,
> refreshing taste of self-reflection.
>
> Happiness Is a Choice—A lovely, hopeful musing whose deep flavors contrast well with the light texture of humor.

She instructed us to take a few minutes to decide what we would like to have for our entree and dessert. We chatted, giddy, and in counterpoint to the serious tone of the event. We came to a decision but without much collective reflection about the implications of our choices. She filled our order as requested by telling two compelling tales.

Performance 3: Paul Cummins interviewed everyone in our class of eight on performing personal narratives. His interview question was simple: How would you respond to someone who felt you didn't do him/her justice in your performance? The responses ranged from "Sorry, but that's the way the performance came to me" to "I wouldn't do the performance if the person objected." When Paul performed, he put everyone in a tight circle. Speaking directly to each of his interviewees, he mirrored what each person had said with all the precision that conversational performance allows. He captured all the gestures, vocal characteristics, and disfluencies that he recorded. He displayed all the skills of a master impersonator. The audience members laughed, loudly, even at times uproariously, except when they were the object of Paul's focus.

I was the instructor responsible for responding to these student performances, and this is my story about these events. It is my story about how these performances positioned me and how that positioning became central to my responses but not always a part of the critical discussions. I start by saying this is a story I would rather not tell. I begin with what I must admit. I wanted Sheryl's story about her parent's death to be true. I wanted Jen to reveal the most intimate details she was willing to share. I didn't want Paul to expose me, particularly if that exposure was to be met with laughter. What sense can I make of these critical responses, these confessions? I do not seek general principles for evaluating autobiographical performances, even if such principles might become evident; instead, I endeavor to put myself on the critical line, to meet autobiographical performance with autobiographical criticism. So I continue by describing what thoughts crossed my mind as I witnessed these performances.

Sheryl's Performance

When Sheryl tells us that her story about her parents is a fiction created for the purposes of having a dramatic impact, my mind goes to two places simultaneously. First, I recognize the moment as an opportunity to lead the class into a discussion of fact and fiction. I know, as Sheryl does about a good death narrative, that the topic, whether fact or fiction, is easy to make work. It is easy to call into suspicion that everyday distinction between the real and the made-up, easy to pull the theoretical threads so that students' assumptions become unraveled, easy to generate heated participation. So, I am grateful to Sheryl for this set-up, this lob waiting for my slam.

But second, despite the theoretical arguments I enjoy maneuvering in the class and despite how those arguments might mock my response, I feel duped, betrayed, and disappointed. I do not, of course, want Sheryl's parents to have died for the sake of the performance. But when I orient myself to the autobiographical performance genre, I expect, by definition and conventional practices, the tales I hear to be tales based upon the performer's real life. I know that the autobiographical genre is not a container in which truth is poured. I know that the self is always being constructed, invented in the moment of its telling. Still, Sheryl took me in. I believed what she was saying was true. Duped, I feel like a fool. I want Sheryl, as I want from all people whom I have no reason to doubt, to tell me the truth. Perhaps more accurately, I want Sheryl to share her version of the truth, and I don't believe whether or not her parents are alive is an open question. Assuming, as I did, that Sheryl would not try to deceive me, I feel betrayed by her lie, by her willingness to break generic expectancies.

Her betrayal worked on me in another way. Assuming initially that what Sheryl said was "true," I felt, rightly or wrongly, that a bond had been established between us. The performance had served as a step forward in our interpersonal relationship. She had shared an intimate detail about her life, and her disclosure seemed to build a connection between us. I felt close to her, felt I understood her better than I had before, felt an intimacy between us. But all that fell apart when she revealed that her parents were still alive. Instead of feeling greater intimacy between us, I felt greater distance than ever before. I became suspicious, unsure what to expect from this person. I heard an alarm sound in my head: beware. The initial pleasure I had in believing that our relationship was deepening was taken away. Perhaps I had no right to think that her performance could offer me a meaningful connection to this person, but, nevertheless, I was disappointed.

What strikes me about these responses is what I elected to discuss in my role as critic. I was quick to put the theoretical issues on the table, and I was also comfortable talking about feeling duped. I did not, however, share with the class my feelings of interpersonal betrayal and disappointment. And if I'm honest, those were my strongest feelings about the performance. Why, then, did I elect to keep quiet about these reactions? I would like to believe that the reason I chose not to share my feelings is because I did not think that it would serve any useful pedagogical purpose or because I was afraid it would place Sheryl in an awkward position, which indeed it could have, given my position of power. But I think the reason that guided my action was less noble: I did not want to share because my feelings placed me in a tenuous position, both from an informed intellectual position and from my ideal relational and pedagogical stance. To admit my feelings would be to point to an inconsistency between espoused theoretical arguments concerning fact and fiction and my genuine response. Moreover, it would have specified a preference for a kind of working relationship between teacher and student that might not be shared. At the time, it would have been to admit too much. But by not doing so, I missed an opportunity to discuss what, if I spoke the truth, mattered most to me.

Jen's Performance

When Jen asked us to select our entree and dessert, we knew what metaphor Jen was putting into play. We knew she was casting us as cannibals. We knew she was making her flesh available for our consumption. By her design, we were caught—we wanted to be cooperating audience members but to do so meant we would have to take on the uncomfortable cannibal role. We would need to push Jen, a person we cared about, into a performance we were not sure how she might handle. Perhaps this accounted for our nervous laughter. But I admit that part of me welcomed the opportunity to dine at Jen's expense.

Jen's performance, then, stirs competing desires in me. I want, first, to make sure Jen is safe, able to present without undue risk the items we select from her menu. I don't want anyone getting cut on the steak knife. Knowing Jen's keen abilities to cook the raw, I assume that she knows what she is serving. But once I decide that is the case, I want, second, to taste the most tender parts. I want to eat the cuisine that I find most appetizing, and I do not want to share with the other table guests why I'm hungrier for some tidbits more than others. As I read over the offerings, I find certain morsels more savory than others, but to argue for those with the other audience members would necessitate sharing more than I wish to disclose. Regardless of my wishes, some edibles position me in a difficult place. Would it be appropriate, for example, for a male instructor to feast upon a female student's plateful of sado-masochism or dish of suicide? I opt for a simple strategy: I use my very best table manners, pretending to have Jen's best interests at heart. In short, I speak without saying anything.

In the discussion that follows Jen's performance, I ask the audience members to share why they wanted to hear certain stories. Their answers are rather innocuous: "I just thought that story would be interesting." "I never heard Jen talk about that before." I do not push them, and I do say that the stories I want to hear say as much about me as they do about the storyteller. I am intrigued and troubled by my desire to select certain tales and by my eagerness to hear them unfold. I do not put these thoughts into the critical mix. Instead, I allow the discussion to evolve into an assessment of the power of her tales. I don't implicate myself. But her performance is about how her audience members are implicated by their choices.

Jen knew, I believe, exactly what she was putting into play. By inviting us to assume the cannibal role, she was offering us a chance to see ourselves. We saw ourselves using Jen as the spice in our cannibal stew, and she allowed herself to be used so that we might be converted. As the performance ended, I knew myself as someone who was willing to come to the table, willing to cannibalize Jen. My only hesitancy was some need to appear appropriate to both Jen and the other audience members. This description, however, sounds too Freudian—the nasty little id being held in check by the prudish super-ego—to capture my feelings at the time. I felt exploitive. I felt sadistic, ready to feed on someone else's pain. Sitting with knife and fork in hand, I saw myself, in horror, awaiting my next meal.

Paul's Performance

The question to ask following Paul's performance was obvious: How did you feel when Paul performed you? Responses varied. Some people felt it was a treat to see themselves done with such skill. Some people acknowledged Paul's skill but admitted to feeling some level of discomfort. Others were clearly disturbed. One student in particular kept asking the audience, "Is that what I sound like? Is that what I look like?" When the audience repeatedly answered that Paul's rendering of him was right on the mark, the student became even more agitated. I, too, was agitated by Paul's presentation, but instead of focusing upon my own feelings about being represented to the class, I noted Paul's skills in capturing all of us so well. I applauded his work and tried to tease out the various theoretical issues that I thought were at stake. I speculated on why the performance generated such laughter by noting the comic potential in recognizing the familiar and in unexpectantly encountering the accurate details of the everyday in an aesthetic frame. I discussed the long history of impersonation, ending with the claim that Anna Deavere Smith's (e.g., 1993, 2000) work is a continuation of that effort. I used some of their own quotes from Paul's performance to encourage them to reflect upon their own responses, particularly those that might increase their sensitivity to putting other people on stage. But I buried my strongest feeling: I did not like myself, the self I saw in performance and the self that was witnessing himself.

From the audience's laughter, I knew that Paul gave the audience a convincing portrait of me. On other occasions students have performed me—quick moments done in good fun—but none with as much duration and detail as Paul's and none staged within such close physical proximity to me. So close, in fact, I was on stage with Paul. I knew I was being watched, and I knew that I was supposed to share in the fun at my expense. Any child who has ever been teased knows that role. But it isn't a role that is very much fun to play. And any adult knows that part of being mature means that you can laugh at yourself. So I was doubly caught: I didn't feel good about having people laugh at my expense, and I didn't feel good about not being mature enough to enjoy the fun. I felt self-conscious, petty, small. I tried in my roles as audience member and critic to hide those feelings, feelings that did not make me feel particularly proud. I also chose to hide the fact that I did not like what I saw—an inarticulate, loud man with an intrusive laugh. I could not object to what Paul had done anymore than I could object to what a mirror might show. I just knew, like the student who kept asking if that was how we saw him, that I didn't much like the self I was seeing.

In retrospect, I believe that I should have disclosed those feelings during the critique. Those feelings offered entry to perhaps the most instructive aspects of Paul's performance. Had I articulated what I was feeling, we might have come to understand more fully what is at stake when giving consent to be interviewed and staged. Even someone like myself who was familiar with the staging of interview materials was caught off guard by what transpired. When I signed the consent form, I was thinking about the content of *what* I would say, and I saw no objections to sharing those thoughts. My focus was not upon *how* I would say what I did. Yet, in performance what I had to say was clearly secondary to how I spoke. Moreover, I did not realize the extent to which I would feel like I was on stage during the performance, not only as a character being presented but also as a witness to that characterization. As a witness, I felt at risk, cast in a role I did not know I had auditioned for and in a role I did not want. Without an opportunity for rehearsal, I didn't trust that the character I knew I was supposed to put on stage. That character was not as carefully rendered as I would have liked. In short, I didn't realize that in giving consent I would have such little control over of the production of my own image.

Facing the Facts

Having put my autobiographical responses into play, having said more than perhaps I should, I try to face the facts, personal facts that make me accountable. Such sharing may lead to a partial discovery of how the autobiographical genre implicates its creators and audiences. Such sharing trusts in the power of a vulnerable self. So, I begin again, telling more than perhaps I should.

As a critic, I don't like putting myself in a vulnerable position, perhaps because I falsely assume that the role needs to carry some authority. My desire to appear as if I have some answers may be what cuts off dialogue, what feeds the ego with illusions, what denies growth. It is academic arrogance at its worst. It is what I've claimed I never want to be.

As a critic, I'm too quick to let theory trump belief and feeling instead of letting belief and feeling question theory. Taken in by theory's pervasive power, I maneuver until I can convince myself that theory writes me. I use its explanations to discipline, to hold me in check, to wrap me up, mummified and dead. I deny truth for theory's easy comfort. I do not cry out as I am lowered into my grave.

As a critic, I want an intimacy without giving anything but an ear. I want to assume that when performers speak of their lives, they speak to me. I want to assume we have a connection. I want more than I am entitled to have. I forget that my ticket only buys what is put on stage; it is not a ticket into anyone's house.

As a critic, I wrap myself in others' pain, silently rejoicing that the performers' pain is not my own. My pleasure comes from the recognition that it is not me who stands on stage, injured, hurt, exposed. I offer a hug and return to the comfort of my home.

As a critic, I tell stories that empower me until they are turned, put under reflecting light, targeted back. Then, they are sites of regret.

As a critic, I negotiate power like a bullfighter working the bull. I wave my red cape with a flourish and hear the applause. I play to the crowd, controlling the moment. I lift my sword before I am ready for the kill. I stand erect and slide by what I must. I avoid the final act of negotiation, the moment when power opens its hand, when all seems equal, when the horn gores the gut.

As a critic, I end believing that to meet autobiography with autobiography is a productive strategy for tapping into what truly matters in the critical dynamic. It reveals how the theoretical and the personal are loaded with desires, with motives, with ideas that genuinely locate one person in relationship to another. Autobiographical criticism, then, is not just about performers' and critics' compelling stories; it's about their telling connections.

Another Case Study

As I come to the end of this piece, questions haunt. As I confessed, how have I positioned readers? Should I ask readers to read such things? What have these confessions done to the writer/reader relationship? Do these thoughts make readers want to push away? What would the readers of this piece like to say?

What if I told readers now that the first performance I described never happened? Would readers feel duped, betrayed? Would readers be suspicious about our relationship from now on?

Have I served myself up, made a cannibal stew?

Would readers mind if I interviewed them about what they are thinking? Would they mind if I put those thoughts on stage? Would they mind if everyone laughed?

Would they have preferred that I put my personal feelings in dialogue with scholarly works, perhaps as a means for holding my confessions in check or perhaps in the name of some grand truths about performing and critiquing autobiographical material? Should I have quoted Hantzis's (1998) concern that personal narratives silence and Gingrich-Philbrook's (2000) objection to that characterization? Should I have cited Heaton's (1998) work where he references "cannibalistic performance" to situate Jen's performance more concretely and, after having done so, connected that work to Alexander's (2000) notion of "generative autobiography," Fuoss's (1999) conception of "performance chaining," and Smith's (1998) description of the "Canterbury Effect"? Should I have built my case from Langellier's (1998) claim that personal narratives should implicate the political? Should I have included Terry's (2006) concern about how such works situate the audience? And so on and so on until, finally, it would have been obvious why I wanted to end using Gingrich-Philbrook's (1998) assertion, "The story takes your turn" (p. 299)? If I had cited all this work, would readers have felt that their time would have been more wisely spent?

Did my modeling convince readers that autobiographical confessions can be a useful critical strategy, or do they think that such confessions are just a self-indulgence designed to pull attention from the performer to the critic? Are readers willing to try confessing, or has this been a part of their critical practice all along?

Did whatever pleasure readers derived from their encounters with this essay come from that perfect marriage, the coupling of sadists and masochists?

Do readers feel burdened by the obligation of it all? Do they insist that this is not what they bargained for? Do they feel resistant, bored, ready?

Would they be willing to share their critical responses? Do their responses take their most meaningful form when they are located in their own autobiographies? Is it their turn?

Criticism

It points to the responsible, offering applause here and accusations there. It swings on the ropes of praise and blame, shimmying up and down before trying to tie everything up in a tight, evaluative knot. Its pointing finger never can undo what it has done, never can unsay the said.

It forms relationships. Like the smiling sycophant, it curries favor. It flatters, it strokes, it kowtows as it tells its tales. Like the sage, it teaches, student to student, in the ongoing quest for the right questions. Like the cool assassin, it sights its enemy, fires, and leaves the dead behind. Like the court jester, it speaks in riddles. It jokes, teases, mocks as it does its tricks. Like the old friend, it tries to explain.

It drops like rain with routine randomness. It lands everywhere. There is no stopping it. Frequently, it comes. It pushes down steady and insistent as an Alaskan air mass. There is no protection, no shelter, no way to weather the daily storm. It keeps coming. It rumbles loud as thunder.

It explicates, but never duplicates. It guides the eye to significant signs, marking what matters. It describes in detail, noting what should be noted, telling what should be told. It keeps what should not be missed from being missed. It plots a course of navigation, drawing lines from point to point. It maps. It knows what it needs to chart.

It excavates, brushing away layer after layer until the buried is exposed. It digs into the dirt. It digs to discover what others have covered. It digs until skeletons speak of the shape of their bones and the color of their skin. It shocks itself by its own discoveries.

It creates dialogue around a round table. It deals out all the cards, face up. Its deck is made of hearts. There are no Kings or Queens, no Jokers, no strategizing Jacks. It will not play battle; instead, it shows its open hand. It shuffles the critical stack, changing the order. There are only high cards. It never trumps. It is without winners and losers.

It pinpoints trouble with precision. With clinical detachment, it operates. Its aim is to save the patient. It dissects, exposing the problem, and then surgically cuts the cancer out. In this sterile, laser procedure, there is no blood, only the conviction that all has been made well.

It theorizes, conceptualizes, problematizes. It perpetuates paradigms and it pricks them. It thinks through thoughts, arguing for or against different positions, answering this or that question. Through deduction and induction, it figures how x equals y, how logical it all is. It establishes litmus tests. It ponders purpose, principles, and pleasure. It puzzles.

It sells. With stars, with dollars signs, with thumbs up or down it gives everything its due. It markets what it likes. It markets, like produce, the labor of others. It thumps and squeezes before it separates the ripe from the rotten. It cashes in whenever opportunity strikes. It sells itself.

It preaches to the congregation, telling of the holy, teaching the good word, gaining more and more converts. It speaks with passion as a faithful witness. It speaks from the soul. It tells the high priests and the lowly worshipers what they should and should not do. It claims what is right and what is wrong, what is good and what is evil. It preaches like an evangelist, like a predator.

It marks a performative moment in memory. It makes histrionics into history and writes people and places into prominence. With a scholarly hand, it fills an event with significance, signaling to all who follow what and against whom they will be measured. It preserves, frozen and unyielding, the presentation.

It celebrates, cheering and cherishing those moments that cannot be wound into words, that seep deep into the soul hot as horseradish. It strikes up the band and hoists up the banner. It is raucous. It cannot contain itself. It wants everyone to know. Yet, it may turn quiet, reverential, soft as a whispered prayer. It shapes the sound of exuberance.

It negotiates differing notions, monitoring the consequences. It does not want to offend. It does not want to hurt. It seesaws cautiously back and forth. Balancing this and that, it watches every turn, every flip, every swing. It carves compromise out of passion. It makes its case by committee.

It stings, like a wanton wasp, piercing deep beneath the skin. Often, it stings more than once. It cures, like a leech sucking blood. It is the pill that cannot be swallowed. It devours, like a starving parasite. It only leaves waste. It only leaves pain. It discards the bones, like a satisfied piranha. It moves on, ready for its next attack.

It turns on its creator. It haunts and obligates. It builds an edifice of shoulds. It carves in stone the critic's hieroglyphics for all to see. It is a monument to the past, to words left in forgotten places, to old habits. It is a reminder that nothing is left behind. It is the Sphinx that awaits its Ozymandias.

It remembers the pleasures of the body. It writes them, pretending that world is present again, pretending, without reservations, that participation is again possible. It remembers how the heart cracks, how it turns, how it pounds. It paints the moon. It permits us to clap, without embarrassment, for Tinker Bell.

Devising

The Process

Devising is a digging down, trying to discover what needs to take shape, what needs must be left in the mud. It works desire like a spade.

Devising demands a readiness and willingness. The half-hearted, cold-hearted, and content-hearted beat against all those who toil heart-to-heart.

Devising disarms the dishonest. It honors the dignity of each participant and asks nothing more and nothing less than an open body. It takes guts to handle, with all its visceral messiness, the guts of the matter.

Devising is a cat and mouse game. The trick is to ensure that the mouse always wins. Find cracks under doorways, dark corners, and drawers never opened. Walls can't shut you out. Let the troubled cat turn to the window.

Devising works by putting bees in your hair.

Devising is a fabric in the making, thread upon thread, finding its design, patch upon patch, stitched together by bleeding hands. It awaits its dye from those who might buy.

Devising, at times, dances into contriving, waltzing with the familiar, two-stepping its way to the obvious, stumbling into predictable form. Choreograph a new jitterbug.

Devising dares to destabilize, to deconstruct, and to destroy the safe designs of our lives. It discovers definition in the debris.

Performance: An Alphabet of Performative Writing by Ronald J. Pelias, 53–61.

The Politics

Devising disturbs with all its questioning, probing. It unsettles as much as it settles. It may pick a fight.

Devising fears the authority of the playwright and the director. It has little room for servants and puppets. It wants an ensemble of voices, each free to speak, each saying her or his own name for the good of all.

Devising delivers by letting the personal be expressed and the political to be argued. It comes fully loaded and piping hot. It should be available in every neighborhood.

Devising is a reaching out, from cast member to cast member, from cast members to those who come as witnesses, in the hope that touch can make a difference in our inarticulate world. It is a circle of sweating hands, joined together, at a time when choosing otherwise is a step toward destruction.

So, why devise, why now? It is a hand to the heart, a fist in the air.

Diminishment

Performance studies scholars are in the habit of casting performance as a method that opens up alternative visions. Whether framed in Madison's (1999) logic of possibilizing, Dolan's (2001) notion of utopian performatives, or some other conceptualization, performance is understood as a way of breaking from habitual ways of seeing, often in the name of working toward social justice. But, when critics enter the scene, the performances of their attention, even those they wish to applaud, may be diminished. Such a claim is not surprising—since Plato first spoke of imitation's limits, critics themselves have been warning just how much can easily slip away. So much so, that the history of critical theory might best be read as a series of cautionary tales about loss. Brook's (1947) protection of the "well wrought urn" by means of the paraphrastic fallacy, Bakhtin's (1981) call for a "dialogic" gathering, and Derrida's (1976) constant, never-ending recovery of the absent, for instance, can all be read as reflections on the adequacy of the critical task. But what interests me most in this piece is how critics themselves may feel diminished by their own practice. The pages that follow outline some of the ways that critics may consider themselves lessened by taking on the obligation of response. My strategy is to identify sites of diminishment by tracking selected moments of my own critical practice, organized around my ability to attend, to apprehend, to achieve, to appraise, and to act.

Diminishment by Degree of Attention

Attending to performance requires a giving over, a surrender, for the duration of the event. It is allowing oneself to enter another world. But entry is sometimes stalled by external forces—the small child that just can't sit still, the crinkling candy wrapper that drowns out the actors, the temperature that turns programs into fans. And sometimes, entry is denied by internal forces. For example, I saw the film, *The Constant Gardener*, a week after hurricane Katrina hit New Orleans, my hometown and where my family was residing, and quite simply, I was not ready to take on the pain and cruelty that the film put on display. After a week of watching the news, I sat there feeling beat up, unable to sink into another tragedy. And when a friend came out of that film crying, I found I could not be fully present to her. Such external and internal factors lead to diminished experiences, and I am diminished by my inability to be fully attentive. But in such cases, while I recognize the diminishment, I accept the unfortunate circumstances and simply lament the loss.

Attentiveness, however, carries other dimensions. Attentiveness demands that what appears on stage is noticed and what is noticed accounted for. I know of no critical position that doesn't assume that the first critical task is to notice. Yet, I have found myself failing to take in props that carried symbolic weight, actions that were key to understanding character, and lines that were essential to a script's meaning. Such instances might be explained away by reference to my theoretical and ideological commitments, my own standpoint, my selective perception, and so on. No doubt, such processes are part of my daily sense-making. But, in the critical arena, I feel them as failures of attentiveness. More often than not, I become aware of my shortcomings during classroom discussions of performances. Students saw what I did not, and as they offer their insights, I recognize what was always there. As a critic who did not sufficiently attend, I am suspect and embarrassed. I carry a sense of "should have." If I were an adequate critic, I tell myself, I should have noticed.

Noticing may not be enough to make one feel confident that one has fully attended. Attending also requires knowing what holds importance, recognizing proportionate weight, and separating the relevant from the trivial. I have seen myself noticing an element of a performance without appreciating its pertinence, without realizing why it necessitated critical attention. One such moment occurred in a classroom autobiographical performance. A self-identified gay student gave a humorous and detailed account of a gay bar scene. Several times during the performance he repeated the line, "But that's a story for another time and place." At the time I read the repeated sentence as referencing the salacious that the performer deemed inappropriate to share in a classroom setting. Only later did I realize that the line, while perhaps pointing to the salacious, was much more about safety and who is licensed to speak openly about their sexual lives. I heard the line but missed its significance and, in doing so, I missed an opportunity to open up an essential dialogue with the student and his audience. I failed them all by my failure to attend.

I have also found myself turning performances into opportunities for advancing my own agendas, whether they might be aesthetic or political. I put on display my full critical wrath, for instance, when performers resist taking artistic accountability in the name of reader subjectivity and freedom. I have come down with such fury on that egalitarian spirit that I have left performances behind. In such instances, I exchange what the performer may feel merits attention for my own interests. Sacrificing the performer's concerns for my own, I am diminished. At best, I am arrogant, coercive, oppressive.

Diminishment by Lack of Apprehension

Failing to attend can be understood as a failure in apprehension. But here, I would like to discuss how the critical vocabularies I do and do not have function as diminishment. When I believe I have a sufficient understanding of a performance, it is because I feel I have deployed a critical system, an appropriate terminology, or a learned set of values. Such an understanding comes at a cost. It pushes what is before me into a logic, a scheme for reading and assessing. And while the structures I have in place allow me to make meaning of the performances I see, I cannot escape their structuring force. I offer my critique based in my own comfortable strategies for sense-making, and then I sit back smugly, having put the performance in its place. But, of course, performances often wiggle when I try to pin them down. So much so, that I am diminished every time I feel I have given a sufficient account.

There are also times when I believe I do not have the critical apparatus I need for sense-making. Such was the case when I saw my first Richard Foreman show. I knew his carefully executed staging, cluttered set, and bizarre characters were meaningful. I knew what I was seeing on stage was purposefully chosen. I knew I enjoyed it. I just didn't know enough to offer an interpretation I could trust. I lacked the theoretical threads that would allow me to stitch this work together. I was not up to the critical task, and I felt inadequate, out of the scholarly and artistic loop, diminished.

Moreover, the critical stances I adopt I contaminate by my own positionality. I am historically and culturally situated, bound by my ethnicity, sexuality, gender, race, and class. I am a carrier of my own infected logics. Such claims, of course, are not surprising; in fact, they feel tiresome, but are nevertheless essential reminders of how easily critical commentary, carrying the infectivity of positionality, may diminish.

Diminishment by Lack of Achievement

Actors on stage accomplish what I cannot. I am often stunned by their abilities, by their vulnerability, by their willingness to give their bodies to the moment. I sit amazed at how they manage and enliven the stage, themselves, and the audience. Every few years, my departmental colleagues in performance studies will decide it is time for another faculty performance hour. I am usually the resistant voice, the one who searches for reasons for delaying the inevitable. But they insist, and I find myself participating alongside artists who can play their voices and bodies like fine instruments. My work, in comparison, is always the thud of a wooden spoon on a rusty tin can. And when the evening ends, I am reminded of my own inabilities, of my own misplacement among artists, and of my own embarrassment. I become keenly aware of and simultaneously lose their accomplishments through my own inadequacy. I read them through a comparing filter that leaves me wanting. I am jealous, desirous of just enough skill that would allow me to stand among them without humiliation and shame. And as these feelings build, I am lessened, not only as a critic, but also as a person.

But before one might ask why such a person would be in the field of performance studies, let me add that I relish the roles of director and critic. I believe I can guide performers into doing good work. I believe I have a keen sense of what makes a performance work. I believe I can help performers become what I cannot be—that is, actors whose actions on stage can make a difference in the world. And, having played the role of director and critic with comfort, I have too easily excused my absence from the stage. I have joked that in doing so, I have been kind to audiences, and there is considerable truth to that. Yet, each time I avoid performance, I become further removed from the demands of the stage, less sensitive to the courage it takes to place yourself before others, and less aware of what I might be asking, in my role as director or critic, of an actor. Each time I perform, regardless of the performance's merits, I am a better director and critic; each time I flee the burden of the stage, I am diminished.

Diminishment by Misguided Appraisal

After applauding myself for the work I believe I can do to aid actors, I must now acknowledge that there are times when I am not helpful, and perhaps, more disturbingly, even harmful. At times, I do not know what is the best thing to say. I do not have the precise vocabulary, the right strategy, or the exact method that will move an actor closer to his or her goal. Other times, my comments cause damage. They may lead the actor astray, disrupt what is working, and, most seriously, undermine the actor, not only in a given role but also as a performer. I wish I could take back the words I said to a friend many years ago when she asked if I thought she should pursue a professional acting career. I told her, as if I had the wisdom to know such things, that I didn't think she was strong enough to "make it." She spent the next two years in a doctoral program pursuing what she did not want before gaining the courage to follow her desire. Happily, she proved my assessment dead wrong as she went on to have a successful television talk show. Only years later did she tell me that my comment put her in that doctoral program. I would like to think that I know better than to say such a thing now. I work in fear of the consequences of my assessments, whether right or wrong. I work hesitant, cautious, and perhaps too aware of the damage I might cause. I work, at times, without honesty, diminished.

But even when I can put aside my caution and be completely honest, my appraisals may not align with the performance. I may offer comments that are clever, complex, and even persuasive to those listening, but miss the performer's intent. My assessment may reduce the performer to an object lesson, a pedagogical prop for my own interests. More often than not, when I am functioning as a critic, I am in the power position. Failing to see what the performer hopes to achieve, I impose my logic on the performance, an imposition that takes away the performer's authority and undermines her or his artistic vision. In doing so, I become a thug, taking what is not legitimately mine.

Offering a verdict, no matter how justified, coolly reasoned, or eloquently made, is an assertion of power. I've heard of an art professor who would call students to the front of the room one at a time on the day their paintings were due. With the student standing alongside his or her painting, he would offer his critique. The student would not be permitted to speak. Once he finished his evaluation, he would announce the student's grade. I do not want the authority or arrogance of such a procedure, although I fear that is, in a more disguised form, exactly what I do. And in the process, whose head have I brought in upon a platter? Whom have I diminished and, in doing so, diminished myself?

Diminishment by Inaction

Performance is often a call to action, a demand placed upon the audience to make a difference in the world. More often than not, I stand in agreement with the performance's call. More often than not, I do nothing. It is not, as Brecht (1964) might suggest, that I feel I have done what I should because I have empathized with the plight of the staged character. If anything, the empathic response I might have often makes me feel greater guilt for not taking action. The individual portrayed becomes increasingly real and present for me through performance. So much so, when I don't act I feel I am being negligent in my responsibility. I am not just failing to act on some principle I have, but I am failing to act on behalf of an individual who has entered my life. I have, when I allow myself to put aside the performance's obligation, let someone down. It is easy, of course, to excuse myself for my lack of action—you can't take on everything; you do what you can; you are only one person; you have to pick your fights. But such excuses often feel weak against the weight of the performance's argument. And so, when I feel I should act, but I do nothing except nod in agreement, I am not the person I want to be.

Perhaps worst, from my position as critic I've told audiences that they should follow the performance's mandates while I did nothing. I have claimed that all right thinking people would be taking action, implying, of course, that I am one of those right thinking people.

Seldom do I confess otherwise. And having falsely claimed the high moral ground, I cast my stones, shaming those who do not heed my word. This is nothing but critical hypocrisy, an embarrassment when I find myself engaged in such a practice.

But even when I do act, I find myself aware of my action's inadequacy. As a critic who has been persuaded by a performance, I might write public officials, carry a sign, or donate a little money. Such actions come with small cost. I wonder if what I do is ever enough—enough for those who may be suffering, enough to alter how we think, enough to change policy. As a critic, I hold a position of social obligation. My remarks participate in a social arena and my actions set examples. Criticism is always an ethical endeavor, a site where I do not always, but always wish to, take on the ethical responsibilities performance puts into play.

Replenishment through Diminishment

I offer this list of diminishments not as some liberal act of self-flagellation or as some plea or desire for a counter-claim, but as a personal reminder of the risks of critical practice. By turning on myself, I hope I can become a better critic, one more sensitive to the insidious ways criticism can harm. I see this self-indictment, then, in the spirit of replenishment, a renewed promise to stay alert to how criticism does its work and how I can avoid diminishing others and myself in critical practice.

Empathy

I want to begin this discussion by describing a personal narrative I saw performed by a woman I will call Leslie. It takes place on a bare stage, except for one white chair, placed downstage, left-center. Leslie locates her story during the time when she was deciding whether or not to have an abortion. Sitting in the chair, her hands constantly rub against one another. She speaks about gathering information about the availability and cost of abortion services in her area, about those she encountered who tried to keep her from terminating her pregnancy, about the difficulty she had in discussing her pregnancy with her parents, about her fears that an abortion might keep her from having children in the future, and about the date rape that led to her pregnancy. As these details unfold, pictures of infants and small children are projected on her body. In the background, right wing legislative efforts to stop abortions are document by a power point presentation. Reverberating with and against these images, she tells her narrative. Her story becomes a moving account of how one individual, trapped between cultural logics, tries to decide if she should have an abortion. At the end of the performance, the audience does not know what choice she made. The performance, however, implicitly makes a pro-choice case.

It is easy to see how this performance participates within a postmodern logic. It carries many postmodern elements—imagistic, intertextuality, undecidibility, and so on. It exists where Owens (1983) claims the postmodern operation functions, "precisely at

Performance: An Alphabet of Performative Writing by Ronald J. Pelias, 63–71.

the legislative frontier between what can be represented and what cannot" (p. 59). I want to talk about how I am situated in this performance on that "legislative frontier." More specifically, I want to place my responses to this performance against what is frequently described as the crisis in representation.

I want to start with my responses, not because I believe that they reflect how the performance should be read or that they have any special claim to legitimacy, but because they are indicative of how someone might react to a postmodern performance. I should say from the onset that I responded very positively to the performance. I could call upon multiple critical positions, from aesthetic to political ones, to make the case of why it earns my applause. What is important here, however, is how this performance situates me as I witness it.

I begin by noting how many postmodern performances function, how they enter my consciousness. Often their power resides in their images, images that remain in my mind as iconic indictments, as critical and compelling complaints. They add force to ongoing discussions. They remind me of arguments I have heard, arguments which implicate me. They force me to think and, sometimes, invite me to take action. They have the potential to change my way of living in the world. Yet, they often seem to obscure the person for whom these arguments matter. I know, of course, that the issues being discussed may matter for a great many people, but I do not meet the person who has to negotiate her or his way around cultural obstacles, who confronts, day in and day out, oppression. The performer is curiously absent. The performer gives her or himself over to stand in for all people who face an oppressive hand. The performer becomes, as Phelan (1993) would happily have it, "unmarked." The body most present is one that functions as a tool deployed for artistic and political purposes. The body most obscured is the one that cries, "This is about me."

Leslie's performance locates itself in the insistence that "this is about me." I hear it as a personal narrative, a tale of one woman's experience. It is a confession, a private experience made public, a painful disclosure. She is exposed. I meet a person, one who continues to struggle with a decision she has made and who has come to believe that no one should legislate her body. She is a person in need and, as I witness her story, I am filled with passion. She matters. I want to reach out, to take action, to help. I think I come to some understanding of her pain and anger. I think I know in some limited ways how she must feel. I begin to feel with her. In short, I empathize.

With many postmodern performances, then, I become engaged in ideas, persuasive political arguments but disembodied ones; with Leslie's performance, I also become involved in a persuasive political argument, but one located in a body in pain, in anger. For me, both can be politically efficacious, but I find myself more implicated by a presence that invites an empathic response and one more eager and committed to take action. Admitting to a preference for empathic engagement sounds a postmodernist alarm, an alarm that strikes three primary bells: (1) empathy reifies presence; (2) empathy reinforces dominant ideology; and (3) empathy negates the desire for political action. What is behind these alarmist claims?

Empathy reifies presence, so the argument goes, through the false assumption that we can embrace others, that we can make others manifest through talk. But presence is only a sentimental desire, a fiction for those too weak to buck up to postmodern reality, too naive to take on the postmodern condition of suspicion. Postmodernism, in its various articulations, often encourages us to live in the "always already," to recognize language's limits. Its interest is to tell what others have missed, but postmodernists are often hesitant to take a stance, for to do so is only an illusion. The other, nothing more than a fragmentary appearance, slips away as easily as speech, unless, of course, it happens to be the elusive person making the postmodern claims.

Empathy reinforces dominate ideology, so the argument continues, because there is no such thing as art for art's sake. It is always for someone's sake. Those who have power control what representations are visible, whose interests invite identification. To make someone present is simultaneously to make others absent. Brecht (1964), for example, strategizes alienation techniques to insure that audiences do not unreflectively accept dominant representations, that they do not mindlessly consume the images before them. His unease about empathy is that representations link words to objects in seemingly naturalized ways. The artist's task is to denaturalize, to defamiliarize political society, calling into question the taken for granted. The assumption here, of course, is that audiences cannot or will not do that for themselves. They are either too stupid to realize that realism might not be real or too protective of their own representations to allow anyone else alternative ones. Audiences, we are to believe, passively take in and are moved by whatever comes their way. They need postmodern guardians to stand at the theatre door to insure no one falls prey to mindless consumption.

Empathy negates the desire for political action, so the argument concludes, because catharsis releases us from political obligation. When the soul is cleansed, all political commitment is washed away. Having cried for the starving children, I don't need to feed them. Having expressed shock at the atrocities, I can go on my righteous way. Having felt for any injustice, I can pat myself on the back and claim that I've done my share. In short, empathizing takes me off the political hook. If I feel for others, I need not act in their behalf. This is essentially why Carolyn Forche (1990) stopped speaking about the political crisis in San Salvado to U.S. audiences. She felt that she was perpetuating a system of commodification and consumption, a system where tragedy is sold for the price of a few tears. But, as Scholes (1992) reminds us, "Texts must be consumed in order to have any power at all" (p. 76), and, I would add, sometimes consumption causes indigestion. Sometimes what I consume poisons and motivates.

Empathy, then, can be framed as a misguided attempt to understand another, an other who is nothing more than a fragment, forever slipping away. It allows those in power to reinscribe their own interests and neutralizes motives for political change. I hope it's clear that I don't find this a particularly comfortable position. It stands in opposition to my own experience, to my own reading of performance. Let me return to Leslie's performance to push the point further.

As I noted, I found myself empathizing with Leslie. Often postmodern performances offer me ideas, separated from an identifiable presence. I may agree with their cultural claims. At times, they present a tight case on behalf of social justice, one that I accept and recognize. They reinforce what I believe. I am not, however, drawn to their speakers. They render themselves invisible and, in doing so, suggest that they do not matter. Leslie, on the other hand, does. Leslie gives me her presence, gives me a particular person willing to share her thoughts. I am moved by the person before me. I come to care about her. I am saddened by what she has had to face. I become angry at those who through word and deed have hurt her. I could resist her story but find myself pulled in by its persuasive power. I am reminded during the performance of those who hold opposite views to my own. Once Leslie's performance ends, I begin the work of placing it with and against other arguments I've heard over the years about abortion. My political resolve gains force. I want to work on behalf of the person I've seen in pain, the person who makes me say, "That's not right."

What, then, might I conclude about the place of empathy in postmodernism? First, the arguments against empathy seem suspect. I need to remain attentive to what actions silence others, to what power structures oppress, to what renders me inert in the face of political wrongs. But it does not seem likely to me that empathy is the problem. Instead, empathy may lead me into the opposite direction, creating space for others to be heard, exposing dominant ideologies, and motivating me to take political action. Villainizing empathy is to take away a vital communicative tool for sharing and understanding the feelings and ideas of others, a tool for coming to terms with the complexity of the postmodern condition, a tool for managing my own position within postmodern cynicism.

Second, some postmodern performances (for example, Leslie's) invite empathic responses, while others do not. Whether a performance does or does not offer such an invitation is not a basis for critical judgment. I find myself, however, drawn to those works that show how ideas have consequences for people. Ideas only matter when they are connected to a struggling body. This is Carr's (1993) concern in *On Edge: Performance at the End of the Twentieth Century* when she says, "When parody and irony are used not to contain emotion but to replace it, they diminish whatever they touch. They allow for no sense of tragedy" (p. 231). Ideas without an experiencing presence provide no reason to stop the floating signifiers. Ideas without an experiencing presence allow me to sit with my hands in my pockets.

Third, empathy may allow dominant authority to see. While it is never easy to recognize whom I might be sitting on, I might just find, particularly when the seat becomes a bit uncomfortable, that I don't like sitting on her or him anymore. Moreover, I may just be the kind of person that doesn't like to sit on anyone. Empathy has the potential, if I am receptive, to help me identify where I'm putting my ass.

Four, empathy can make things matter. Perhaps I'm only restating what I've previously said, but I want to end on a personal note. I want to make my body present in the insistence that empathy can make things matter. Leslie's performance elicits my empathic response and, in so doing, calls me forward to act in the social world, to insist on certain rights for women. Equally important, her performance calls me forward as a friend to any woman who may face the same difficult decision Leslie did. If that happens, I want to remember Leslie's performance for how I might fail, how I might attempt to legislate her body, how I might say things that cause pain. I learned how I want my body to be present. I learned that I must keep the person behind the ideas present.

Epigraphs

The paper I wanted to write was entitled "The Possibility of Performance Errors and the Critic's Accountability." Each time I would begin, and there were many beginnings, to write this piece, I would outline a series of arguments I planned to make. I would decide on a persuasive structure, line up citations for support, and anticipate what objections might come forward. I would be convinced that the essay I was about to write had promise. And then, time after time, I thought I could just as easily argue for another perspective, that my commitment to the ideas before me was at best ambivalent, that my allegiance was wavering. I could not bring myself to push arguments forward that didn't carry the force of my conviction. What I do believe, however, is that my understanding of performance errors comes to me from a multiplicity of positions, logics, and theoretical regards; from a historical, cultural, and personal situatedness; and from a career of witnessing. I cannot shove one argument forward without diminishing other positions I hold in equal regard. Frozen by that realization, I offer a series of epigraphs on performance errors, epigraphs that could serve as the basis of a more traditional essay.

> What is found by language's pointing is never innocent. What is lost by language's usage lives in the cracks between words. What is gained by language's claim is determined by desire.
>
> Paradigms produce performance errors. Positioned and paralyzed by their own logic, right and wrong pledge their allegiance to each position's postulates.
>
> It's the fluff, the vacuous entertainment, offered on behalf of passing time in the company of the mindless. Applaud loudly so you cannot hear yourself think. Applaud loudly so you can assume you've gotten your money's worth. Applaud loudly for the pleasure of clapping.
>
> Mistakes matter when the possible is left behind, unfulfilled.
>
> Fiddling forfeits fidelity, an error for those who care about texts and for those who claim authorial rights. Be forewarned, following your folly is a flimsy freedom.

Performance value is calculated by the positive moments remembered minus the errors seen. "A" equals "almost" and "B" stands for "because" in the algebra of it all. The final answer is dependent upon the unknown quantity of "X."

Clarity is the obligation of artists and audiences. Art is never free from its burden.

The door that fails to open. The line that is dropped. The yawn that competes with what is being said. No retakes are allowed. Being live is to live in error. Being alive is to live in error.

Rehearsal pushes errors away but never promises complete protection.

There are basics: adequate volume, sufficiently lit, remembered lines, and so on. Failures here are considered amateurish, unprofessional, blunders. All else are choices, some considered errors based upon artistic preferences and personal biases. Some just don't work, and all one can do to explain why is to say the word art.

Make choices, be precise, polish—the performer's pursuit, the critic's chew.

Craft easily gets everything in the expected design; art's difficulty is to discover an arrangement of desire.

Named errors become wounds, some minor, some not. They reside in the ache.

In the face of error, compassion saves face.

Even after the announcement, the cell phone light will flash; an audience member seeks a connection beyond what is right there.

Going through the motions—the performer who recites lines based only on a rehearsed memory of how they should sound, the audience member who pretends to listen, the director who calls upon a ready bag of tricks—leads to no motion, no emotion.

Error equals damage felt.

Liability is error's terror, its ethical estimate.

Fault finding is an easy task, a habit sometimes deployed as a strategy of self protection; but, in actuality, it denies the self what might be gained from a labor of generosity. Finding what's of worth is worthy work.

Error is mapped by already made charts.

Pointing a finger at oneself can be a bid for forgiveness and an obligation.

Positive responses to errors are a watery soup, served perhaps with kindness, but offering little sustenance.

Errors are the least happy choices in the realm of possibilities.

The distance between "must" and "might" is the artist's madhouse.

Good reasons and bad reasons generate applause. Knowing the difference is the critic's curse.

Being wide of the mark is a reminder that the bull's-eye belongs to those who are responsible for its location.

Theatrical mistakes are to be taken in as moments to be taken away. They are actions found guilty.

Performance's error is in its disappearance; performance's value is in its continual appearance. It thrives on excess.

Figure

Performance figures its way through:

Metaphor

A link, a generative, explanatory model (for example, Burke's [1945] dramatism; Goffman's [1959] everyday life presentations; Turner's [1974] social dramas; the playwright's drama) comparing everyday and staged actions, seen as mirroring (mimesis), making (poeisis), and changing (kinesis) human behavior (for example, Conquergood, 1995), requiring "preaching to the choir" (Miller and Roman, 1995) because there is value in looking at and generating support for a better made mirror and in expanding the choir before discovering, after the mirror's work is done, that it needs to be altered once again.

Synecdoche

Partial, never the whole, a reduction by necessity, by choice (Hudson, 1973), by violence (Bogart, 2001), an incomplete completed sounding that sounds complete, but never is; always a single offering, anticipating the next enunciation, the next claimant, the next bodily form.

Metonymy

An associative shadowing, a contiguous echo, a relational haunting (Strine, Long, and HopKins, 1990) that stands alongside, pointing back and beyond; a reminder ricocheting here and there, until meaning is made, claimed, tucked away like a possession or until ambiguity is the holding point, the celebration of the possible.

Performance: An Alphabet of Performative Writing by Ronald J. Pelias, 73–74.

Personification

Embodied, from the page—sound from silence, flesh from ink—a translation of the page's form to the body's form, perhaps similar, perhaps not (Bacon, 1972), always, in the performer's hands, "writable"(Barthes, 1977), regardless of how open or closed (Eco, 1976), displacing the arrested with the alive (Long and HopKins, 1982).

Hyperbole

An exaggerated declaration, an embellishment with over-reaching claims insisting on its extended reach, its power, its effect, but never knowing just what it does as it does its business, as it makes its flamboyant case—never knowing, like any of the arts, just where it sits on the entertainment-efficacy loop (Schechner, 1985).

Oxymoron

A tensive and productive conundrum, a double bind (Peterson and Langelier, 1982), knowing itself as a fictive fact, a truthful lie, a doing undone (Butler, 1990, 1993; Searle, 1969), an appropriate appropriating (Johnson, 2003), a material immateriality, a present absence (Derrida, 1976), and a living death (Phelan, 1993), knowing the pretense in its real articulations, the unraveling of the woven, the taking and the giving, the consequences of the fading, the tangible in the missing.

G

Generative

"We create, we know, and stake claims to and about ourselves, others, communities, technologies, and cultures in and through performance." (Bell, 2008, p. 27)

It started as I glanced at the front page of my local paper. Pictured was a young white boy dangling his feet in a cool stream on a hot August day; a sixteen-year-old white girl who had won a music scholarship to Julliard holding a flute to her lips; and, on the bottom of the page, a school picture of an eleven-year-old white girl who was the victim of first-degree murder. Allegedly, two black boys, ages seven and eight, committed the crime because they wanted her bike. The details of the murder were graphic. A few weeks later, I discovered, buried on page nine of the paper, that the two accused boys were forced to confess to a crime they did not commit. This juxtaposition of images grabbed me, disturbed me. I felt the weight of race in these accounts. I wrote a poem about meeting these stories, about injustice. I started collecting other newspaper accounts that told of some horrific act that one person had done to another (for example, a woman kills a pregnant woman so that she can take her baby, a man molests two young children, a mother stabs and leaves her one-year-old child in a schoolyard dumpster, a man who when discovering he is with a transgender woman beats her until she is paralyzed, a model is attacked with acid by a man she briefly dated), acts often located in the dynamics of race, gender, class, or sexuality.

Performance: An Alphabet of Performative Writing by Ronald J. Pelias, 75–78.

I wrote more poems and eventually pulled the poems together for a production entitled *Headliners*. I wanted to put on display a case via the negative. I wanted to stake a claim in the obvious: People should not treat each other this way.

"Performance is dynamic and generative, enabling difficult and controversial stances and poses that ultimately help us better to articulate our objects (and subjects) of inquiry." (Johnson, 2003, pp. 6–7)

I've always loved T. S. Eliot's poem, "The Love Song of J. Alfred Prufrock," even though I've known Prufrock's world is a privileged world. Given both my love of and discomfort with the poem, I decided to stage it, first by presenting Prufrock's world as written and then by allowing five performers who claimed an identity outside of Prufrock's privileged culture to insert their own resistant reading of the poem. For example, to Eliot's lines, "... there will be time / To prepare a face to meet the faces that you meet," D. Nebi Hilliard interjected:

> Surely not the face of the honey-roasted complexion of my great-grandmother. "Aunt Sarah" they called her. "Nigger whore" he called her each time he raped her when the missus was away. Her weary eyes ingested more acts of hate than her drawn, full lips could ever relay.

Following Eliot's line, "Arms that are braceleted and white and bare," Denise Menchaca inserted:

> White arms? Does he mean pale? Translucent? Downy? Milky? Fair? Light? Ivory? Creamy? Luminescent? Or does he mean pasty? Pallid? Drab? Colorless? Lifeless? Dull? Ghostly? Sickly? Waxen? Lackluster? I do know he didn't mean brown or coffee-colored or tan or caramel or sunburned. He didn't mean arms the color of my grandmother's, cinnamon, dusky, bronze.

The cast through personal stories, quick commentaries, and witty remarks offered a counter-point poem, a poem they felt had much more resonance for and in their own lives. After adding their own words, the cast wanted to drop presenting the poem without their additions, but I, as the white, male director of the show, insisted Eliot's words first be spoken without interruption.

"For a performative autoethnographer, the critical stance of the performing body constitutes a praxis of evidence and analysis. We offer our performing body as raw data of a critical cultural story." (Spry, 2011, p. 19)

My intent was to create a dialogic opening for the audience when I directed *The Academy* for the National Communication Association convention. The script, compiled from the writings of communication scholars, presented a picture of the struggles and joys of academic life. In this hard and celebratory look, a cultural story emerged based in the life experiences of academics. It came forward as an ethnographic glance, a snapshot from the inside. For any number of reasons, it came forward without generating much response.

"Audiencing autobiographical performance often triggers in me memories, images, and glimpses of my own experiences." (Alexander, 2000, p. 97)

As I watch Lesa Lockford's one-person show, *Lost Lines*, I am carried to her grandparents, billed as "The Marvelous Lockfords" during their vaudeville days, pulled to those lost years before Lesa was born. I am carried to Lesa's mother, now in her eighties, who recently moved from her home in Los Angeles to live next door to Lesa in Toledo, moved into her last house, moved to a place of care. I am carried to the edge of a river, represented on stage by a small pool of water, where Lesa remembers her grandmother as she empties the ashes of her grandmother's husband, and where Lesa imagines she will let the ashes of her mother fall. I am always with Lesa in her moments of love and sorrow, and I am with my family, remembering my dad's passing and my mother now in her nineties.

"A radical performative pedagogy politically and ethically means putting the critical sociological imagination to work. This work involves pedagogies of hope and freedom." (Denzin, 2006, p. 335)

It was a short essay, called "Straight and White," written by W. Benjamin Myers, a member of an eleven-person ensemble cast that generated texts about their bodies, and staged in a show I directed entitled *My Body*. Every time I saw the piece in rehearsal I would laugh. I couldn't stop myself. It was so wrong, and, I think, right. Ben's piece used the idea of working for straight and white teeth as a way to mock the privilege of straight and white bodies. In staging the piece, I had three straight-and-white men and three straight-and-white women pair up and form a line upstage center. I asked the five cast members who were not straight and white to take varying positions downstage from the straight-and-white pairs. After dividing the lines among the straight-and-white pairs, I instructed them to move forward together delivering their lines with as many smug, self-satisfied smiles as they could muster. I further instructed them to walk over or through the non-straight-and-white cast members as if they were a bit of an inconvenience, as if they weren't there, as if they were invisible. It was so wrong, and, I think, right.

"I believe that theatre and performance can articulate a common future, one that's more just and equitable, one in which we can all participate more equally, with more chances to live fully and contribute to the making of culture. I'd like to argue that such desire to be a part of the intense present of performance offers us, if not expressly political then usefully emotional, expressions of what utopia might feel like." (Dolan, 2001, pp. 455–456)

I write and perform two anti-war poems. The first, "How to Stop the War," presents an Iraqi teenager standing on the rubble of his bombed home, howling for his buried family, waving an AK-47. The second, "The Flag Ceremony," is told from the perspective of a father who is presented with an American flag for the loss of his son who was killed in action. Against the ongoing tidal wave of the U.S. military complex, this is perhaps a small ripple, perhaps not.

Holy

1.

"The theatre must recognize its own limitations. If it cannot be richer than the cinema, then let it be poor. If it cannot be as lavish as television, let it be ascetic. If it cannot be a technical attraction, let it renounce all outward technique. Thus we are left with a 'holy' actor in a poor theatre" (Grotowski, 1968, p. 41).

> *A stripped body before us, vulnerable, making an offering, is a holy act, a penance on behalf of us all.*

"I am calling it the Holy Theatre for short, but it could be called The Theatre of the Invisible—Made—Visible: the notion that the stage is a place where the invisible can appear has a deep hold on our thought" (Brook, 1968, p. 38).

> *An insight, shared, unfolding before us, is a holy act, a collective body taking communion, an act carrying the taste of change.*

2.

Brothers and sisters, we are gathered here today to welcome these new members into our flock. They have been trained. They have shown their willingness to sacrifice themselves in the name of others. They have studied the holy books and have listened with care to the revered amongst us. They have participated in many sacred ceremonies, showing their skills to command the belief of the witnesses before

Performance: An Alphabet of Performative Writing by Ronald J. Pelias, 79–81.

them. They have given themselves in the name of all we call holy. I now ask all of you to step forward.

Do you swear that your salvation depends upon your commitment to stand on the pulpit of representation?

I do.

Do you swear that you will honor your commitment in both body and soul?

I do.

Do you swear that your belief is strong enough to withstand meager shelter and subsistence?

I do.

Do you swear to put no other calling before you?

I do.

Given the powers invested in me, it is my privilege to present you with the frond of the palm: The branch, a symbol of the arch that separates and brings together; the leaves, a symbol of the multiplicity of possibilities; and the wind it makes as it passes from my hand to yours, a promise of what is to come.

Let us all now offer our spirited applause.

3.

"Using the language of spirituality often seems to be an attempt to wrestle with concepts that are difficult to grasp.... Spirituality obfuscates rather than illuminates aspects of the ephemeral. Their inherent resistance to specificity makes terms such as spirituality and sacredness hard to engage critically. Thus, rather than aiding inquiry, they hinder it. There is little room to hold the terms up to the necessary, or any, academic and theoretical rigor" (Myers, 2012, p. 165).

Towards a series of possibilities for holy research:

> The holy in performance is a resting place, an occasion to pause in the glorious mystery of it all, to relish the ineffable, to embrace the unexplained.

The holy in performance is a hoax, a lie we tell ourselves when we want to believe in something beyond ourselves, when we fumble forward without understanding, when we try to convince ourselves that what we do is meaningful.

The holy in performance is an elusive horizon, identified as a place to go beyond the mundane, a space to be reached only through a god's helping hand.

The holy in performance is an ethical trap, promising purification while it perpetuates purgatory, each purge another punishment, each purge another empty pledge.

The holy in performance is the embodied word, from the body to the body, a sharing devoted to communal clemency.

The holy in performance is holy.

4.

The gospel according to Stanislavski, Craig, Meyerhold, Strasberg, Artaud, Grotowski, Brecht, Hall, Barba, Brook, Miesner, Schechner, Foreman, Le Compte, Boal, and Bogart, to name just a few: DEVOTED PRESENCE.

Imagination

I am teaching Kim Stafford's (2003) book, *The Muses Among Us*, in my Writing as Performance class, and I find his call for the writer to see himself or herself, not as a prophet, but as a "scribe," a "secretary to the wisdom the world has made available" (p. 5), particularly seductive. I start a daily journal to listen to life's "perpetual feast" (p. 17).

Following Stafford, I devote myself to the "passing fragment" (p. 26). I yield to what is given, striving to become a "connoisseur of whispers" (p. 32). After a number of faithful days of playing the scribe, I fall into what one day's entries want to be, lean toward what voice is struggling to be heard, embrace the coherence that is born from life's random abundance. That day of record is trying to teach me how the imagination works in our lives, in our work.

I arrive on campus early, enter the Communications Building through my usual backdoor, and start to ascend the stairs when I see it: Three rock sculptures, one placed in the middle of each of the three concrete benches in front of the building where the smokers often reside between classes. I exit to examine more closely. Gray as the benches, each consists of perhaps ten palm-size stones, collected from a nearby garden, elevating to a height of ten to twelve inches. One delicately balanced on top of the other, the stones, simply standing there, seem to have emerged from the benches, as if the benches, weary from their years of utility, decided to believe in art. With the sun filtering through two protecting oaks, I feel calm, invited to stop

Performance: An Alphabet of Performative Writing by Ronald J. Pelias, 83–108.

before my day begins. I stand there, smiling, steady over the crack in the cement. From out of nowhere, Phillip, a student of mine, appears.

"Sometimes," he says with a touch of embarrassment, "I just have to do something like this."

"It's beautiful, Phillip," I reply. "Thanks for doing it."

"This morning I just knew I had to do something." I do not inquire why this particular morning demanded such an action. I simply nod, accepting that what Phillip says is true.

Sometimes, the body insists that the imagination do its work because it needs what the imagination can conjure.

Throughout the day the sculptures are the talk of all who pass. No one, even jokingly, attempts to knock the stones down or push them aside. No one fails to pause. The benches, once a place for flopping fatigued bodies, are surrounded. Non-smokers are invited into the circle. The once unremarkable space becomes marked with questions of authorship, aesthetics, and appreciation. Two maintenance men going about their chores stop by what appears before them. One moves to the center bench, leans in to examine the stones, then announces: "It's art." Then, convinced of his assessment, he says again with finality, "Yes, it's art," and walks away seemingly satisfied.

Sometimes, the imagination takes a form we recognize and, only then, do we know what we are to do.

When the day has reached its end, I see that the stones are no longer stretching upward but are in small, collapsed piles. I am sad. I go to the benches, mourning, and, perhaps in a desire to recover what has passed, I lift one of the rocks, feel its rough texture, notice its flat surfaces. I sit with weighted memory. Before long, I begin to stack and discover how easily one rests upon another. Soon, my quick work uses all of the little boulders, replicating what stood before. I am disappointed. I push my trivial tower down and head for home.

Sometimes, imagination's grind lies in its ideas and sometimes in its making.

My wife has been planning to take a one-night piano class at the local community college designed to teach a particular chording technique. On the designated night, she has second thoughts. "Do you think I should go?" she asks. "I'm worried that the class will be so full that it won't be of much value."

"I'm sure they will limit enrollment to manageable numbers," I offer.

"Maybe," she says, sounding as if she is more persuaded by her fears than by my optimism. Thinking that she'll regret not going, I give it another try.

I'm sitting here re-reading Kim Stafford's chapter entitled, 'Live or Die,' for class tomorrow. I have to say 'Live.'"

"I think I'd prefer to take a nap." She leaves—I assume to take a nap—only to return twenty minutes later, bag in hand, ready to rush out the door. "I decided to go."

Sometimes, the imagination waits for us to take our turn.

I greet a graduate student in the hall, a student who has been struggling in the program but who has my full support. After we exchange pleasantries, her tone changes as she says, "I put a letter in your box, and I want you to know that a decision has been made." Then she hurries off. I sense that the letter will not bring happy news, but I don't know what required the formality of a letter. I return to my office and find her letter of resignation. It is brief, a simple statement that she will not be coming back in the fall. No explanation is given. Later that day, I see her again.

"I got your letter. It made me very sad."

"Thanks." After a short pause, she continues, "My husband and I have been talking and talking about this for a long time now. Last night we stayed up to four a.m. thinking through all the possibilities. We looked at our situation from every possible angle until we knew this was the right decision."

I nod, trying to understand.

"This whole thing," she says, gesturing to her surroundings but implying much more, "just isn't working for us. We tried and tried to make the pieces fit—they just won't come together."

Having been told earlier that further discussion of this decision is not welcome, I simply say, "I'm truly sorry. We will miss you."

Sometimes, the imagination, exhausted, demands a stop.

Tara, another student, one I hardly knew, also saddens me. I had received an e-mail from her several weeks before my summer course began. She wrote:

> Dear Dr. Pelias,
>
> I have enrolled in your summer course but because of a job I have I won't be able to attend on Fridays. Is it alright with you if I miss those days?

Knowing that the class is a four-week intensive class that meets every day for two hours, I wrote back:

> Dear Tara,
>
> That would be quite a bit of class to miss—the equivalent of missing eight classes in a regular semester. See if you can find another way of working out this problem.

She answers by saying that she'll try to just miss the second half of class on Fridays. I write back suggesting that I still see this as a problem, but perhaps we can work something out. I receive no reply. Class begins and Tara does not appear on the first or second day. On the third day, Tara arrives after the first hour, just before our break ends. She introduces herself and asks for a syllabus. "Tara," I say, "you've already missed so much class and with your scheduling problems on Fridays, I don't think it would be wise for you to take this class."

"Are you saying that you don't think I will do well in here?" she questions.

"Not with how much class you've already missed and with how much class you will miss because of your job," I say. She turns, offers a sigh, and leaves. Later that day, I receive another e-mail:

> Dear Dr. Pelias,
>
> I think it was very unpleasant of you to tell me that you did not think I would do well in your class. I feel you did not give me a chance and for that I think you are being very unfair. I feel you did that for a specific reason, one that I won't name.

I feel the weight of her accusation, implying that once I saw that she was African American, I thought she wouldn't do well.

Always, the imagination, like all language, travels with its own ideological baggage.

Over lunch, several friends and I are talking about writing. We discuss how journals and diaries carry gender associations, how the process of recording daily thoughts and images may help or hinder other writing, what freedoms we allow in the notebooks we keep. I mention that I've kept a journal for years, always the red and white mottled Mead composition books, bound by black tape. "I use it for quotes I read and particularly like," I say. "Kim Stafford's book," I add, "has inspired me to become an 'eavesdropper' in the world, to keep another kind of journal."

"I've kept a diary," a friend shares, "since I was eight years old. I stored volumes in my parent's basement. On my last trip home, I thought I'd look at them, but I discovered that water had found them. They were ruined. The ink ran together—page after page of black and blue water colors."

"The same thing happened to me," another friend confesses. "I had been keeping a journal for years before I discovered that my husband was secretly reading them. I felt so violated I took all my journals, wrapped them as carefully as I could, and buried them on a friend's farm. Just this summer I decided to dig them up. But the elements got to them. The pages were stuck together, mildewed, moldy—they couldn't be read."

We all sat there, quiet, thinking about loss.

Sometimes, the imagination's record, no matter how hard we try to preserve it, turns back to the world.

I give my students an exercise to help them see how improvisational acting can help their writing. Their task is to create a short play using improvisational techniques based upon the following situation:

> Assume that you are a same sex couple living together in a committed relationship for the last three years. One tension within the relationship, however, is that one partner has never acknowledged to his or her family that he or she is living in a same-sex relationship. The tension comes to the surface when an invitation to a sibling's wedding comes to the house addressed to "Fran (or Dan) and Friend."

The students embrace the exercise and produce several engaging scenes. We select one to workshop, and after several improvisational turns, decide on an ending we feel works. The play quickly moves into a heated debate filled with accusations and threats between the characters. By the end, the characters are reduced to one or two word responses.

Jan: Now?
Fran: Yes. What?
Jan: Nothing.
Fran: No.
Jan: What else?
Fran: Us.
Jan: Hard.
Fran: I know.

The scene stops without resolution. We are left with two exhausted boxers, wounded, each in her own corner with nothing left to give.

Later, I'm telling a colleague about this classroom exercise and indicate my surprise and disappointment that all of the plays contained similar themes and similar points of conflict. "Did any of the plays put the partners in a supportive role with each other and make the family the point of conflict?" he asks.

I shake my head. "No, not a one," I say, wishing I had thought to improvise this variation.

"I would say," he continues, "that's a failure of imagination."

Sometimes, the imagination, working within its limits, settles into its diminished capacity.

I read the Kim Stafford line, "We take dictation from the world" (2003, p. 19), and it strikes me as familiar. Trying to place it, I think it might be from Wallace Stevens. I go to the books on my shelf and spend the next hour and half looking for what I don't find. I have other things to do, so I have to abandon my search. Later, though, I encounter a colleague whom I trust to know such things. I explain what is haunting me and ask if he might be familiar with the quote. He ponders for a moment, but nothing comes forward.

"Are you going to be around for a bit?" he asks. I can tell he doesn't like not having the answer. I indicate that I will be, and an hour later he returns.

"I haven't found it yet," he says, sounding disappointed in himself.

"I didn't mean to give you a job," I reply, disturbed that he has spent so much time pursuing what I should be chasing. "I just thought you might know."

"Well," he says, resigned to his fate, "now you've put it in my head."

Sometimes, the imagination assembles what it can't accomplish.

The imagination, then, is a trickster, leading me to my biases and limitations and giving me puzzles I can't complete and can't let go. It is a taskmaster, insisting on my presence, my daily work, even when it accepts that I must stop. It is a voyager, discovering its form, its ideas, or discovering itself lost. It is a saver, always trying to hold what it has found. It is a lifetime companion, welcoming my attention. It knows that Kim Stafford is right: The Muses are among us. My charge is to listen, to record, and to see what the imagination might do.

Insufficiency

Even now I want more; more of what I have carried with me for many years whenever I thought about Craig Gingrich-Philbrook's show, *Cups*; more of that love story between Craig and his partner Jonny that had planted itself in my head in full bloom; more of that feeling that the love between two people transcends dogma and hate, even if dogma and hate take daily negotiation; more of that faith in Gingrich-Philbrook's words to educate, to calm fears, to make us better people. You see, I want my memory of Craig's show to be sufficient, not an enigma. I want Craig's show not to have the subtitle, *Sufficiency Enigma 1999*. I want to believe that how the show has worked on me over the years was sufficient to the show. But desire, though it may live in the comfort of its own privacy, exposes its vulnerabilities whenever it speaks beyond itself. So, with hesitation I write, not only compelled to explore *Cups: Sufficiency Enigma 1999*, a show I love both in my memory and in my current encounter, but also to reflect upon the insufficiency of memory and the enigma of its accompanying desires.

The Sufficiency of the Incomplete

Gingrich-Philbrook starts the show with a statement of desire: "Even as a boy, I wanted more." The "more" he wants takes us beyond the young boy on his bike feeling the curve of the road and lying in the lush meadow with his dog resting in the crook of his arm, beyond the "sad stories" of his troubled home, beyond his dead brother and estranged father to a place where he could "just be there," perhaps with Andy, his boyhood friend, or with someone else who might find him "sufficient, 'enough.'" He wants to language that desire, to use autobiographical performance as its articulation, despite knowing "we each sit, lonely, isolated, trying to collect ourselves, to compose ourselves after bad dreams in which the love comes to nothing, drinking coffee from our battered cups." He wants to know what a broken cup can contain.

He tells all of this in front of the curtain after being guided out by the stage manager to the light. It is as if he has been placed in police line-up, asked to step forward, and to confess. And we know he has a story to tell. But before he is willing to share his tale, he informs us that this will not be another of those stories we have come to expect from him. It won't be all neatly packaged in the aesthetic of repetition, autonomous, separate from our lives; it won't move forward without fear; it won't speak as if death has had its say. The curtain opens and he enters the world where the tension between more and enough becomes the enigma of various encounters.

In this world's first scene, Gingrich-Philbrook rolls up his sleeves, his signature gesture, mirroring the action of a waiter in a New York café. He had gone to the café to write about death, "about having had enough death" in his life, at the urging of his partner, Jonny. He finds himself in the middle of a performance, the performance of the waiter who works the room by pouring coffee into empty cups with the folksy charm of porn star Al Parker and the potency of a newly dominant male zebra that aborts with his highly functional penis all the pregnant zebras so that he can "reinseminate the 'empty' zebras with himself." The waiter emerges as both oppressor and seducer. As oppressor, he imposes his will upon those present, filling them up, like the zebra, with his performance, erasing their identity as they are cast into the role of the receiver of this presumptive heterosexual display. As seducer, his performance has appeal—its physicality, its efficiency, its sexuality:

> As he raises his arms, he pulls that worn t-shirt out of his jeans, up like a curtain. An inch or so of his white boxers show, too, marking all the stages of dress and undress in a small territory: his bare skin, his underclothes, his shirt, and jeans. He's somewhat tan, and, though this structure of revelation would be enough to momentarily catch my eye until civility led me to turn away, I glimpsed his small yin and yang tattoo, rising like a moon about the edge of those boxes. And, in the final moment of this transformation, the thin trail of hair leading from his navel into his pants caught along the length of forearm, tripping the hair along the edge of me like so many hundred alarms.

Gingrich-Philbrook, despite the attraction, places his hand over his cup, signaling "no more," and leaves a tip, "wondering if I've left him, wondering if I've left him enough."

In a different register, he then asks the audience:

> Did you like that story?
>
> Where do you want to look? What do you want to happen?
>
> Are you glad I didn't act on my attraction toward him? Do you want me to stay faithful to Jonny? Do you think about Jonny? Do you want me to hook up with the waiter, Jonny be damned? Or do you want the waiter for yourself?

And in the asking we are confronted with our first enigma, our first encounter with the issue of sufficiency, of what is enough, of what our cups might contain. The tale is left in questions, projecting alternative endings. It stands as a fiction in this moment's telling, as a refusal to let death take hold. It is, as Gordon (1997) would have it, a story of hauntings and ghosts.

Embedded in the waiter's story is another tale questioning sufficiency. Gingrich-Philbrook tells of another encounter he experienced when searching on his hands and knees the bottom rack of a poetry section in a New York City book store. An unknown man, head bandaged from a recent operation, appears above him, breathing heavily, his arms extended in anticipation of a hug. This moment takes him back to a dream of his father who returns, like Lazarus, from the dead only to die again. Remembering his father, Gingrich-Philbrook hugs this bandaged stranger, a hug of gentleness and comfort, a hug of connection. Then, a therapist emerges, pulled forward by a dog on a leash. She says:

> Is he bothering you? I'm sorry. He won't hurt you. He's recovering from brain surgery. He has a little brain damage. They love everybody when they have brain damage. They love everybody at this stage.

They continue their embrace a moment longer, separate, and the strange man takes Gingrich-Philbrook in "like he knows we'll never see each other again." Then, escorted by the therapist, the bandaged man leaves, offering a brief wave once he reaches the door. Gingrich-Philbrook tells us he "never had the dream of my father again." The hug he gives the bandaged man and the hug he gives his father, the audience is invited to believe, is necessarily sufficient and not enough. Perhaps brain damage is what is needed.

Gingrich-Philbrook's next story revolves around his decision to move away from New York City and from Jonny for a job in Carbondale, Illinois. As his New York friends express their concern that a gay man won't be safe in southern Illinois, he remembers the inscription carved in marble in an Illinois bathroom stall: "KILL FAGS." As he relates this, a light comes up on a sign positioned in the aisle to the audience's right. It reads, "KILL THE AUDIENCE." He speaks of living a life in fear, sharing his own feelings about sitting in that stall, offering a moment of reflection for Matthew Shepard, bringing forward his own and friends' stories of narrow escape and stories of those who didn't, including a southern Illinois man, Michael Miley, who was "killed and beheaded and burned in his car." The scene ends with Gingrich-Philbrook saying that he has no intention of killing the audience since he isn't in favor of killings, public or private, but that "none of us are all that safe, really, when you think about it."

The sign, "KILL THE AUDIENCE," served to make the audience experience the weight of living under that cultural script for just a few moments and, perhaps not surprising, proved to be a highly contested performance choice. For some, the response to Gingrich-Philbrook's statement, "I hope that sign wasn't too much," was that it was too much. They were, in short, unable to get beyond the audacity of the threat. For others, the sign created an instructive site of implication where the audience could acknowledge their own participation in a horrific cultural logic. In a reversal of the previous scenes that locate the sufficiency enigma in the desire to want more, this scene foregrounds the desire to want less—less of those who are not like us. It ultimately asks if killing and, more directly, "killing fags" would be sufficient to satisfy hate.

The final scene returns to love's sufficiency as Gingrich-Philbrook tells of his move to Carbondale without Jonny. The tender and loving labor of their decision to live apart and of their separation at the train station is juxtaposed to the cultural stereotype that gay relationships are empty, void of genuine feeling. Gingrich-Philbrook then reclaims empty—that feeling you have when apart from the one you love. That feeling is exemplified most fully in the story of cups, favorite cups exchanged so that "we could, in a way, still have breakfast together." Unfortunately, when Jonny comes to visit, Craig's cup breaks, leaving only broken pieces. Gingrich-Philbrook shows the audience a piece of the broken cup. It is half a cup, handle intact, jagged.

> I hold onto this piece of broken cup, this handle I couldn't hold onto when it fell beyond my reach. I keep it in a jar on my windowsill, where it rubs up against other shards of other broken stories. With the rest of them, it catches the sun in the morning, the handle, and the hollow, and the lip of it, warming and cooling with the course of the day.
>
> And though it can no longer hold water to the standards of the material world, it has never, since he picked it up and put it back in my hands, been the slightest, been the slightest bit, been the slightest bit empty.

This broken cup, then, is and is not sufficient, is and is not enough. Its insufficiency, however, seems to slide away against its fullness. It becomes desire's best, although incomplete, answer to more. This cup tells what a cup can contain. It knows that the shards that can slice open are what keep death at bay.

The Insufficiency of the Complete

My memory's failure was to let death in, to give closure to the show's enigmas. *Cups*, as I remembered it, was a love poem to Jonny, a poem so articulate, so tender, that it rewrote what I understood love to be. It was a display of the power of language to name what slips away, of words to tell passion's secrets, of metaphors to reveal what may be present in the equation. It was a story of pleasure, a story that gave me pleasure, real and complete as a rose. It was all that, and, as I hope the section above demonstrates, much more. After revisiting the show, I know I must reluctantly surrender memory's settled tale, that desire for more of the same, for memory's tale to be sufficient. Memory, as *Cups* now instructs me, is not enough.

When Craig moved to Carbondale leaving Jonny still in New York, we spent the day together looking for a place for him to live. Craig was most attracted to an old neighborhood with modest homes, many serving as student rentals and many showing their years of hard use. We looked at dwellings with tilting floors, with porches hanging on by the sheer willpower of a few nails, with sheds that could become performance spaces, one only big enough for an audience of one. I kept trying to lead Craig to newer neighborhoods, to more upscale places where not long ago there were cornfields. These were houses freshly painted, clean, efficient, ready for occupancy. But Craig would always have me circle back to the old neighborhood. Perhaps his attraction was to the large trees shading the streets on that hot August day, the easy access to campus, or the familiarity of the area from his graduate student days. But, more likely, it was to the homes that held their history, the ones that didn't determine their use, ones where shards of glass rest happily on the windowsill. We never found a house in that neighborhood and settled on a place somewhere between our two desires. When Jonny moved to town, they found a place together in that old neighborhood.

I have always been too easily seduced by the tidy. I live trying to keep everything in its place. And, when the dust settles, I am content until some troubling finger disturbs the pattern. Then, if I can, I wipe clean, restore a new order. Postmodern Craig might roll his eyes at this modernist admission, but, more likely, he would ask if the dust can ever really settle or, if it does, settle evenly; if what we call dust, like language, is simply a way of disguising and defining what is there; if we can talk about the dirt that is left behind after everything is wiped clean. In other words, he would more likely remind me of the easy slide from dust, to dirt, to death. I write to dust over what disturbs, to be done; Craig writes to disturb the dust, to begin. And that is perhaps why I allowed my memory to have its way. I wanted Craig in the safety of my construction, secure, gathering fairy dust. I wanted Craig in the house without ghosts, without hauntings. I wanted Craig in the loving arms of Jonny. But *Cups* teaches me that such desires take daily labor, that just when we think the dust has settled, another finger will leave its print. Nothing comes clean.

Usually, about twice a week, Craig will come into my office, our shared home, and we will chat for an hour or so. We'll talk about our current projects, students that we celebrate and worry over, and the latest idiocy of the current administration, both on campus and in

Washington. I cherish our time together, just the two of us, talking. There is a comfort there, him sitting in the chair always ready for his arrival; me, across the desk, leaning back, taking him in. There is a devoted and loving comfort in that collegial exchange, although I always feel he has much more to offer than I do. There is a comfort in seeing him there, like me, just talking. Less often, I go to his office. When I do, I am always welcomed but, more often than not, he has to clear a space for me to sit. Perhaps the clutter is intentional, a way of being cautious, a way of deciding who can safely be let in. I am, quite honestly, more comfortable when we chat in my office. And that, too, may be why my memory storied *Cups* the way it did. It is easier for me to have Craig come to my office, come to my place of comfort. It is easier for me to read Craig like me.

For a while, Friday nights were movie nights. With our partners, Mimi and Jonny, we would often take in the latest release that Carbondale, Illinois, managed to get. Afterwards, we were off to Denny's for a bite and conversation. Usually we would start by talking about what we had just seen, but before long, Jonny and Mimi would begin tracing the actors' previous credits, their favorite scenes from another film which, of course, is a homage to another film which was the third in the series by such and such director whose last film appeared seven years ago, only because he was able to land such and such actor for the lead who had already appeared in two films that year with co-stars so and so, who… Craig had the skill but not always the inclination to join in. I was usually lost after the conversation left what we had just seen. Sometimes, during such conversations, Craig and I would catch each other's eye, wanting more. When we would depart, we would hug, I believe, with love. Mimi and I would return to our tidy, cream-colored walls, comfortable, safe; Craig and Jonny would drive to their overloaded book shelves holding the weight of the read and unread, to their half-finished craft project awaiting their hands, and to a broken cup, so full, on their windowsill.

Sufficiency Enigma Once Again

Any essay that wishes to applaud necessarily comes forward as a broken cup, filled with the love it knows how to give. It is never enough, never sufficient. Such a claim, of course, is only to repeat the postmodern warning of language's slippery deceptions and unachievable dreams. Moving forward with postmodern caution, with the skeptic's eye for language's tricks, with the predilection to disrupt easy pleasures, it becomes difficult, if not naïve, to celebrate when language satisfies. But, *Cups* does satisfy, both in my original reading and in my current one. So, I am left as a critic who writes of *Cups*, insufficiently, trying to tell of *Cups's* pleasures, trying to offer in words a sufficient account, trying to deny what postmodernism teaches. Despite my effort, I find myself wanting more. But ultimately, the more I want is Craig's to give. I want Craig to say, "Enough."

I long for the "enough" I imagine Jonny felt when he listened to *Cups*. I see him there in the audience, sitting erect, nodding as Craig moves through the piece. He is taking the show in, like food, like a lover's touch, like salvation. Even now, whenever the show is referenced, a knowing smile crosses Jonny's face, a smile that remembers how the show names their love, how it says publicly that they are connected, regardless of how others might wish to narrate them. But that is too much to ask. Instead, I must content myself with my remembered encounters, to settle for my own sense of "enough," to relish my own satisfactions.

I am sitting there, head cocked to one side, leaning in, not wanting to miss a word. I know I am in the presence of something special, something magical. The show whispers in my ear. Others in the audience drop away. It is speaking to me, telling me what everyone, myself included, needs to hear. I am in the café, watching the waiter maneuver among the tables, coffee pot in hand. I am on my knees in the bookstore, looking up to a stranger who asks for nothing more than a moment of human contact. I am in the bathroom stall, reading "KILL FAGS." The language carries me along, placing me here and there. I listen to it turn, turn again, and turn back on itself. I applaud its elegant work even while it works on me. I am inside and outside its construction, amazed, taken.

I watch Craig, his sleeves rolled up, moving on stage. There is a quiet there, a softness, an invitation. It seems as if his body is always full front, although that is not actually the case. It seems as if his voice is some combination of a cat's purr, a glide in the wind, and the deep beat of a drum. He is a panda bear, a peeled grape, a cracked acorn. And he speaks to me, sharing what I imagine he wants to say when we talk over lunch or in my office, but never quite does. I trust what he says as if it were my own blood.

Cups is, as Phelan (1997) would have it, a rehearsal for death, but not because it offers a neat closure. Instead, it allows death in because, and I do not exaggerate here, it is impossible for me to imagine anything better. It comes to me as an argument, so richly nuanced, so carefully articulated that my understanding of love is forever changed. It comes to me as a poem, so finely crafted, so elegantly stated that I am stunned by its electric current. It comes to me as a gift, so generous, so right that I am incapable of responding in kind.

So, when the show ends, I greet Craig with an embrace. I stand there holding him, not wanting to let go, not wanting this moment to end, and I utter what I can manage: "Oh, Craig. Wow!" When we separate, I leave saddened and elated. Only later do I recognize myself as a parasite to a host, feeding, taking but giving nothing in return. I write now, insufficiently, in the spirit of a return, wanting more—more skill, more grace, more Craig than I am capable of conjuring. I will crumple these pages and place them on my windowsill.

Investments

I speak to students and students speak to me, sometimes coming closer, sometimes pushing away. We language our relationship together. At the beginning of the semester, we mark our desires, that often change with each utterance, sometimes fulfilling promise and sometimes leading to disappointment. As the semester unfolds, I find myself making different investments with each student. In this piece, I track those investments across seven students who enrolled in one of several beginning Performance of Literature courses I've taught. Putting on display my relationship to these seven students, presented here under pseudonyms, I show my ideological, theoretical, practical, and personal investments. In doing so, I foreground my own emotional interests and my own failures. In short, I am writing to take stock.

As I proceed, I work from the belief that the best teachers can motivate and inspire students to do their best work, that they can turn student indifference into a love of a subject, that they can shape students into better people. I want to be the teacher who Hart (1993) applauds, one who thinks, feels, and acts; that is, one who has more questions than answers, who is concerned about social justice, and who is a "maker of people" (p. 100). This belief, one that I've never been able to shake after many years of teaching and after reading scholars (for example, McLaren, 1994; Alexander, Anderson, and Gallegos, 2005; Fassett and Warren, 2007) in critical pedagogy who suggest that the troubling logic of my stance can find its way to hubris. It works against the notion of teacher-student interaction as a dialogic engagement where both teachers and students have agency in determining their educational goals. What I see as a pedagogical failure, a student may understand as a satisfactory accomplishment of his or her desires. Even so, I hang on to my belief and turn to those students I might have worked with differently. I want to give an honest account of my own processing, maneuvering, and investments, not to scratch some narcissistic itch, but to uncover the troubling ways I dealt with some beginning performance students, students who continue to haunt.

Troubling Investments

Drew

I first met Drew when he needed my signature to return to school after being suspended for poor grades. He assured me that he was ready to turn a new leaf, that he knew he had not taken school seriously before but was ready now to do the work. I have heard such claims many times. Sometimes they are true, sometimes not; but I gave him the needed signature and sent him to our departmental advisor to sign up for courses. Drew was specializing in public relations but discovered that all the public relations courses he wanted were closed. He found himself signing up for my Performance of Literature course.

After I gave the first assignment, Drew asked, wanting to get it right, "What do you mean by performance?" Given where we were in the semester, his question surprised me. Drew had never missed a class, and he seemed to be taking careful notes.

I answered: "Remember how we've been talking about becoming the speaker in the poem? I want you to say the words of the poem capturing all the attitudes and feelings of the speaker. Does that make sense?"

"I think so. Do we have to move around?"

"Think through what the speaker of the poem would do. Match your actions with the actions of the speaker," I said, feeling tired. Two days later, Drew came to my office.

"Would you mind looking at my skit before I have to do it for class," Drew tentatively inquired. I had given this option to the class, and Drew was the first student to act on it.

"I'd be glad to, Drew, if you promise never to call your performance a skit again," I said winking, hoping to make a playful corrective to a labeling that matters to me perhaps more than it should. We found a rehearsal space, and Drew did his performance. It was clear that Drew had worked, that he was trying to incorporate the suggestions from class. But the performance was not strong, even by beginning student standards. After working together for about an hour, it was better but still not strong. I gave him some goals for his future rehearsals, and when he did it for class, it was even better but still short of what one might hope. I applauded his growth. This pattern continued with each of his performances, and I grew increasingly fond of Drew. I enjoyed working with him, moving him along, incrementally, slowly. He was always prepared when he came for his tutorials, always eager for suggestions, and always willing to laugh at himself and try again. Our sessions together were fun. To be honest, though, by the end of the semester, Drew was not a significantly better performer than when he began. He had little affinity for performance. At best, he might be cast as the third crowd member from the left. I wish Drew well. I hope he has a good life, and I hope he left the class with some appreciation of literature and performance. He did leave with a well-earned B. I do not know, however, if he felt our investments yielded sufficient dividends.

Ann

Ann had the look of a young undergraduate student who was president of her sorority rather than a student who worked in a local bar, but six nights a week she poured drinks until 2:00 a.m. This was not a happy work schedule for a student with a 9:00 a.m. class. When she came to class, she was exhausted, hardly there.

One day when Ann and I were the first to arrive to class, I said, directing my comment to her head resting on the desk top, "Ann, I'm worried about how much class you're missing and when you do come, that you seem half asleep."

"I'm sorry," she answered, lifting her head from the desk. "I work at Gatsby's, and by the time I get home, it's two thirty or three o'clock. If I have homework to do, I don't get to bed sometimes until five or six."

"Ann, that schedule is a killer. It surely can't be good for your health and it surely can't be good for your school work."

"I have to work to go to school," she said, resigned to her own entrapment. I've seen other students caught in a forty-hour or more work week, trying to cover expenses, trying to carry a full class load. They take on some pay-the-bills job so they might go to school, but the pay-the-bills job eats away their ability to do school in any meaningful way. Ann managed a low C in the class, but I believe she learned little. She made another step toward her degree, in her goal to become licensed, but did little toward her education. Ann reminds me how different students arrive in our classes with different financial backing, different systems of support, different chances of being the students we want and the students they want to be. Too often, I invest too little in students with limited opportunities who are not performing as the student I desire.

Kiyomi

Kiyomi was a student from Japan whose English skills were not what they should be for taking a class in English that did not have a textbook. As might be expected, she seldom spoke during discussions and when asked if she understood a point, she would nod. I became increasingly suspicious that she did not understand what was expected of her for the class. "Kiyomi," I called, catching her after the class was dismissed. "Do you know what you need to do for the next performance?" She nodded.

"Good. Try explaining it to me," I encouraged.

"What?"

"Explain the assignment to me so I'm sure you've got it right."

"You want me to memorize a story."

"Yes, a scene from the story you select and I want you to apply the principles we have been discussing into your performance," I added. Kiyomi nodded.

"Do you know what I mean when I say that?" I pushed further.

"Yes." Kiyomi seemed to become increasingly uncomfortable with my probes.

"Okay, then. I'm looking forward to your performance," I said, ending what was a painful exchange for both of us. Next class, Kiyomi handed in the title of her selected text.

"Are you sure that is the text you want to perform?" I asked. "The narrator of that text is a Mexican American who speaks with a distinct accent."

Kiyomi nodded. When Kiyomi's turn to perform came, she recited her poem, but nothing more. I applauded her ambition and talked about the difficulties of performing in a second language, particularly when the language being performed was unlikely to be the form of the language that she was taught. I asked her to return to the stage, as I often do with students following their performances.

Wanting her to realize that she might embody the narrator's actions, I pointed out a place where I thought the narrator might sit.

"Let's just try these three lines. I want you to sit after the first one," I said, trying to give her a task she could accomplish.

"You want me to sit there and say the words," she asked.

"I want you to sit after you say this sentence. Then say the next two sentences," I said, pointing to the sentences from the story. She began but, becoming increasingly nervous, she could not get through the first sentence. "That's okay. Try again," I encouraged. In her next attempt, she offered a mangled version of the sentence, stopped, looked at me, looked at the chair, looked at me again, and seeing my nod toward the chair, went to it and sat.

"Can I go to my seat now?" Kiyomi asked.

I nodded and tried to make amends: "I know this is hard, particularly when you haven't had a chance to rehearse what I'm asking you to do." And perhaps it was too hard for Kiyomi. She stopped coming to class. Investment, without a shared language, is bound to diminish in translation.

Tasha

Tasha, a very talented performer, wanted to go to graduate school because she wanted to be in a place where she could continue to perform. "I'm happiest when I'm on stage," she would often say. But when the Graduate Committee saw that her GPA was below the minimum requirements for admissions, her GRE scores in the single digit percentiles, and her letters of recommendation signaling caution, they moved quickly through her application to more promising prospects. As the Director of Graduate Studies, it was my job to notify Tasha of the decision. I knew she would be disappointed, and I knew the decision would affect her behavior in our class.

"Tasha, I'm afraid I have some bad news," I said, trying to sound supportive. "The Graduate Committee did not support your application for admission into the graduate program."

"What?" She seemed surprised, stunned.

I wasn't sure if she didn't understand or if she wasn't ready to accept what I had said. I repeated the news, this time more directly: "The Graduate Committee said no to your application."

"You can't do that to me."

"I'm sorry, Tasha. I know this isn't the news you wanted, but do know that the Graduate Committee had to say no to many strong applicants. It was a very competitive year." This was language I have used before—it allows me to hide behind the Graduate Committee when in actuality I am in part responsible for the outcome. I doubt if it offers much comfort. Tasha was not comforted.

With a tear slowly moving down her cheek, she stared right at me. "You did me wrong," she said, stripping me of my Graduate Committee protection. She turned and walked away. I did not see Tasha again. She stopped coming to class. I sent her several emails but received no reply. I heard she returned to Chicago. "You did me wrong" are the last words I have from her. I still believe Tasha was not a good investment for our graduate program, but I wonder how Tasha might understand such a judgment knowing that I said following one of her performances, "You are such a talented performer!" I wonder if I led her to invest in that identity. I wonder if I may have taken it away.

Alison

Alison was perhaps the most disconcerting student I've ever had in class. She spoke only when addressed directly or when it was her turn to perform. She never missed a class, never took a note, and never took her eyes off me. It was her eyes that were most troubling. For sixteen weeks, she stared. She stared as if she were performing what she thought good student behavior might be. She stared as if she were looking through me, as if something on the other side of me was her interest. She stared as if she were somewhere else. She stared as if everything I said was unworthy of response, meaningless. She stared as if she were incapable of any other expression. She stared as if I were a fool or guilty of some unnamed, heinous crime. She stared, and I struggled to understand, to make some sense of what she might be thinking. She gave me nothing that would allow any interpretation I might have to come to rest.

I found myself trying not to look in her direction, but in a small class, that strategy was difficult. I tried not to let her stare bother me.

I would say to myself that her stare had nothing to do with the class or me, but I could never convince myself that was the case. I would attribute her stare to her own oddity—she's just like that; she's a bit off; she's in need of help—but again, I could not narrate her so easily. Her work in the class was solid, not the best but surely not the worst. She must be getting something from the class, I would think, and then I would reconsider—perhaps she already knows what I am attempting to teach and she's bored.

I decided to talk to her outside of class, to ask her how she was processing the course. I made an appointment with her, but she didn't show up. "I missed seeing you for our appointment yesterday," I said to her before class started.

"Sorry," she replied, staring right at me.

"Well, let's figure out another time," I said, but we never did. Perhaps the thought of facing her stare more than the three times a week I had to was more than I wanted to endure. But I did know that we had no connection, no teacher-student relationship, no joy in learning together. With each class, my investment diminished. Rattled, I had nothing to give.

Nick

Nick brought to class his high school forensics training. He knew how to chew a line and how to find the drama in a piece even when it wasn't there. His performance work would often impress the class, and I would face their resistance whenever I offered Nick more subtle or text-based options. To Nick's credit, he was always willing to try whatever suggestions I might have. During work-throughs, he would do what I asked, but he never stopped watching the audience's reaction, he never stopped hearing the audience's applause from his own choices. Nothing I said spoke louder than their appreciation.

I liked Nick. He had a quiet charm about him and a keen intelligence that he guarded. I saw in him considerable potential until the day we ran across each other and started chatting about the class. "Where did you go to high school?" I asked, wondering about his forensics background.

"Carbondale," he answered.

"Did you work with Mr. Berry?" I pushed on.

"Yeah, I was on the speech team for four years," he said with pride.

"My daughter was on the speech team when she was there. My partner and I directed a show for Mr. Berry."

"What were her events?" he asked.

"She did dramatic duo, poetry, and prose. What were your events?

"Dramatic duo, original comedy, and oratory," he said.

"I bet you won your share of rounds."

"Yeah, I got to state finals in oratory and I won a bunch of stuff at regionals," he said, smiling.

"That's terrific, Nick."

"It was a lot of fun."

"You know, Nick," I said, feeling it was time to take a risk, "you really are quite a performer when you leave some of that forensics training behind."

"I know that is what you want me to do," he said.

"Forensics teaches some terrific skills, but it often comes with some problematic baggage," I offered.

"Well, I get what you are trying to teach me in class, but, to be honest, I really don't care. I mean, I just like performing. I don't like having to think about it," he responded with more candor than I anticipated.

I laughed. I didn't quite know what to say in the face of "I really don't care." I finally offered, "Well, I appreciate your honesty." We parted, and with that parting my investment lessened. I continued to push my agenda with Nick in class, but he felt like someone I should have won over but had lost.

Janet

Truth be told, Janet was my favorite student in the class. She was an English major who loved literature, who wrote the best papers and exams in the class, and who took her work seriously. She, however, had never performed before. But what she lacked in technical performance skills, she more than made up for in her ability to recognize the demands of a text. She knew what behaviors a text called for even if she could not always execute them. Her performance choices were smart, insightful, never off base. As the semester progressed, her performance skills improved, but like any beginner, she still had much to learn.

My pleasure in watching Janet throughout the term came from seeing an intelligent person working to learn a new vocabulary, a new way, for her, of thinking about literature. My pleasure came from her pleasure in learning, from her ready acceptance that performance is a legitimate way of studying texts, from her eager willingness to test her ideas in performance. My pleasure came from our shared belief in what we were doing.

My pleasure in having worked with Janet only increased when the next semester I learned that she was taking another performance class. "That's terrific, Janet. I'm so glad you're in there," I said to her.

"I just find that I like how the people in your department talk about literature more than how the people in English do," she responded.

"That was my experience as well," I said.

"I was thinking about going to graduate school in English, but now I think I want to be over here," she said, showing her excitement about the prospect of joining the department. I was equally as excited. It seemed a minimum investment had paid off well beyond my expectancies. She made me want to invest more, to offer as much as I have to give, by simply saying that she wanted to join those of us who place our faith in performance studies. She had said the magic words that call forth maximum investment.

A Closing Portfolio

Taking stock, I feel little pride. My investments should have been wiser, more carefully studied, executed with greater skill. For Drew, I should have held on to my belief in a liberal arts education, to trust that the time we shared together was time well spent. For Ann, I should have remembered that students come to the classroom with disparate challenges, disparate demands on their time, disparate possibilities for being present. I should be present to them. For Kiyomi, I should have pushed beyond our language differences, should have reached beyond what often keeps people apart, should have found a language that would have allowed us to connect. For Tasha, I should have guided her more carefully to her strengths, shared alternative options in keeping with her abilities, allowed her to keep her dignity. For Alison, I should have looked beyond what disturbed, seen what she was saying in her stare. For Nick, I should have allowed him his theoretical commitments, held mine in check, and taught him how to grow within his own legitimate beliefs. For Janet, I should have proceeded with caution, avoided zealous proselytizing, been leery of quick conversion.

Despite recognizing what I might have done, I fear that my future investments will follow similar paths. I do not know if I will be able to resist those students who seem to offer the greatest potential for growth, the greatest promise of profits measured in terms of my own desires. I do not know if I will be open to those who do not value the same stocks that I do. I do not know if I will only fully invest in those who love what I love, who want to join the ranks of us dedicated to performance. I do not know if I will get beyond my own interpersonal inadequacies, ineptness, and limited capacities. I do not know if I will move beyond my own ideological, theoretical, practical, and personal baggage. I do not know if I will make the proper investments.

Judgments

Photography

My Mother's Photographs

My mother sends me photographs of our last family Christmas from the Photoshop program she installed on her computer. We are all there: my sister's three teenage boys hanging on my father, each vying for the next moment, each focusing on him while he, in his Santa's hat, looks toward the camera; my mother, sitting at her table, watching, ready for conversation while she cuts up celery and carrots for the dip; my brother and sister-in-law, she kissing his cheek, happy after two drinks and after all the good years of marriage; my sister and her husband, she smiling, having found a place to be; my wife and daughter, trying to please the camera's eye, wondering where they might fit in; my brother's two boys talking together, almost forgotten in the corner. We are all there, red-faced, grainy, and printed on paper too thin. We are all there, needing the gloss of photography, the smooth shine that tells us to hide the pictures that didn't come out right. We are all there.

Robert Mapplethorpe

It is the children that disturb. It is those faces without lines, just discovering shame. It is those small hands trying to cover themselves. It is those children who look forward, asking.

Performance: An Alphabet of Performative Writing by Ronald J. Pelias, 109–123.

Bubbles

On the mantel, you can see a photograph of my daughter, age three, lying in the tub, her face surrounded by bubbles. Only her face, slightly off-center, is pictured. It seems to float there with her brown brows and brown eyes turned up slightly and her lashes wet and black. You see her little nose. You see her skin without a blemish. You see her rose lips curve into their perfect shape around her mouth which is slightly open, showing her straight white teeth, showing her sweet smile. Barely visible, you see her tongue, not ready to show itself, preparing in the dark.

Across the room, I see now my much older daughter studying hard the chemistry of her day.

Joel-Peter Witkins

I look in horror at the bodies with missing parts, with extra parts, with tormented parts; to the masked and exposed bodies; to the strapped, tied, and crucified bodies; to the sado-masochistic bodies; to the patched, scratched, and twisted bodies; to the bodies residing in the surreal, the phantasmagoric; to the deviant, aberrant, and eerie bodies; to bodies, demonic and angelic; to the mocked bodies of famous and broken art; to the sad, weak bodies, suddenly unhidden; to the bodies of desire. I look at these bodies, still, afraid I am seeing myself.

Painting

In the Museum

I feel the cool air as I enter, even in the midst of the hum of all the bodies lining up, crisscrossing, in a hurry to take it all in. I pay so that I can see what's beyond the old guard. Sometimes, I head straight for the special exhibition or to the museum's most famous holdings; other times, I go directly to the display of my favorite period or work; still other times, I plan how I might proceed without wasting a step in order to see as much as I can within my allotted time. Having made my decisions, I move forward like an ant in search of food. Today, I head for the impressionists. I decide against the headphones designed to tell me more than I have the patience to learn. I pass the tour guides, often talking in front of a large canvas in a language I do not understand. I pause by an English speaking guide for just a moment to hear what she is saying, to see where she is pointing. Then, thinking I don't want someone to tell me how to look, I move on.

I find the wing I want. I begin to mill slowly around each room, but I am too excited to linger in front of any one painting. Some paintings I recognize; some I don't. An unfamiliar one catches my eye. I do not know whose painting this is. I stand there, looking, but, given my distance from the wall, unable to read the name plate. I move closer so that I might see whose work this is. It is a Paul Cezanne. I pull back to look again, embarrassed that I did not recognize what I should. I pull back, weighted with history. I pull back, now knowing its worth.

Later, I will stop in the Museum Gift Shop. It will be packed with art connoisseurs buying postcards, posters, and tee-shirts so that they won't forget. I will wait in line for the cashier.

Paul Delvaux's "The Village of the Mermaids"

The mermaids sit erect on straight-back chairs, staring straight ahead, stunned, empty, their long, plain dresses resting on the narrow dirt path outside their small rooms. Their deep blue and gray dresses cover their arms, collar their necks, and keep their tails from view. Their hair is long, running down their backs; their hands rest on their laps. Eight can be seen, but the eye believes there are more around the bend that leads to the sea. In the distance, almost unnoticeable, a man, dressed in top hat and waist coat, perhaps carrying a black cane, walks past the last pictured mermaid. Still further down the path, more mermaids, hardly visible, undressed, some lying on the beach, some diving into the water. The village itself appears carved from the white mountains. On the left side of the painting, a shadow smothers the white mountain which seems to stand guard over these legendary sea creatures. Against the blue sky by the sea, another white mountain marks the coast.

What stories am I to tell, standing there, looking? What tales run through my mind? Should I sit beside the mermaids wondering if their emptiness comes from being pulled from the sea; if they long to return to the ocean floor, to their mermen, to where their tails bring no shame; if they stare from the shock of being placed on display, of being used, of learning the tragedy of their magical fate? Should I resent the male figure, see him as a symbol of bourgeois oppression, see him as responsible for the mermaids' plight, see him as judge of it all? Do I think he is filled with desire as he moves beyond the available mermaids toward those on the beach, unavailable, yet to be captured? Should I see myself walking alongside him? Should I wonder what I might feel walking alone down that path? Should I be afraid to make eye contact, afraid that conversation might crack their mask-like faces, afraid of my own desire? Should I imagine myself carrying one into her room, undressing her, becoming thick with passion but puzzled, having no legs to spread? Should I try to intervene, try to take one after another to the sea, try to free them so that my Disneyland world can safely return? Should I resist judging?

On My Walls

On the walls of my house, I have Monet, Degas, Rodin, Doisneau, Toulouse-Latrec, and Van Gogh framed behind glass. Made into souvenir posters, they stay in place. Seldom do I notice them.

Sculpture

Claes Oldenburg's "Spoonbridge and Cherry"

I've never seen "Spoonbridge and Cherry," but I have a postcard of it pinned to my office wall. It shows a giant white spoon aching over the water to a small rock island before turning up to hold its red cherry with black stem. The postcard is from a friend, Chris, who, after seeing the Oldenburg retrospective at The National Gallery in 1995, selected a picture of what she hadn't seen to send her greetings and to remind me of her upcoming dissertation defense. Scope is everything.

Paper Clip

The meeting seemed to drag on and on and I was stuck in a room with no escape for at least another thirty minutes. It was too small of a group not to give the illusion of interest. So, I found myself twisting the silver paper clip that once held together the papers for our gathering. First, it was a simple, thin "s," tall and straight as a Buckingham Palace guard. With another slight twist, half rested on the desk and the other half reached into the air. Bending out its arms, I turned it into a coiled snake, ready to strike. Flipped over, it showed its geometric lines, four almost of equal length, connected but running in opposite directions. With geometry in mind, I made it into a triangle, although its top was more rounded than pointed. I opened its base and tilted it back and thought that I might market such a design to hold a book in the perfect position for reading. I improved the design by turning one prong forward, but then I realized I needed another paper clip to duplicate the design so that two prongs would face forward and two back. Without ample supplies, I abandon my entrepreneurial enterprise. I started wrapping the paper clip around my fingers. I sensed I needed to look attentive again, so I wrapped without looking, just feeling its shape. After a moment or so, it was knotted, the metal at certain points stressed, agitated. I dropped it from my hands to the table, and there it was, my sculpture, possessing all that I was feeling.

Venus di Milo and Me

Holding my arms behind my back, I stand in the Louvre studying the Venus di Milo, the goddess of love and beauty. I realize that from a certain angle, my arms appear as if they are missing, one just above the elbow and the other right at the shoulder. Her weight rests on one foot; my weight rests on one foot. Her shoulders are slightly rounded; my shoulders are slightly rounded. Her robe hangs on her hips; my jeans hang on my hips. She stares; I stare. Form is everything. We are nothing alike.

Rock and Seagulls

I know for a sculptor it would be the equivalent of a Hallmark Card for a poet—excessively sentimental, trite, unimaginative. But those three bronze seagulls coasting beside that dark rock had an appeal. Perhaps it was because I could lift the gulls from their connecting base and place them higher or lower on the rock; perhaps it was because living in southern Illinois I needed some connection to deep, never-ending water; perhaps it was because it represented one of the few things I had left from my first marriage. So, about a week after tossing it out, I began to miss it.

The Top of the Stairs

Since everyone who needed to go upstairs in the Communications Building would have to pass there, we had a long habit of posting announcements on the wall for club meetings, bake sales, and performances. There, birthday banners were hung, directions to various offices were arrowed, and other messages were tacked to catch the passing eye. So, when I was told that the university had commissioned a sculptor to do a work for that space, the cynic in me spoke: "Oh, great, that will just teach our students that sculpture is a place to tape announcements." But I was wrong. Perhaps it is because of the power of the work or perhaps because students know enough to respect art even if they don't appreciate it. Whatever the reason, nothing can be found there now except a set of smooth, black, circular shapes and straight lines against a white wall, the dark metal and empty spaces of the sculpture pulling the eye—no, pulling the body—as one moves slowly up, higher and higher, to the top of the stairs.

Theatre

School Plays

To comfort a faculty member who was having trouble with a production, the chair of the Theater Department said, "It's just a school play in the middle of fucking nowhere." It was a thought of such comfort to her faculty that they had it printed on a sweatshirt for her when she left.

Paint Boy

In a series of performances, the paint boy (Keith Pounds) would place tape over his mouth, center himself over a large canvas, situate himself on rollerblades, suspension ropes, or a tricycle, and connect himself to ropes that extended to the audience. The demands of the performances on the audience were clear: Manipulate the ropes while the paint boy would squeeze paint onto the canvas. Surrounding the paint boy, audience members would pull his ropes, would pull against one another, yanking the paint boy here and there, causing the paint boy to fall, sometimes violently, onto the canvas. Before long, the paint boy and the canvas would be covered in paint. The paint boy stopped these performances when he decided the pain was too great, when paint boy began to think of himself as pain boy.

In my office, I have two pieces of canvas from two different performances hanging on my wall. In front of one is the paint-covered tricycle. I sometimes glance up from my desk and wonder when art is a reminder of pain and when pain is a reminder of art.

Musicals

I always leave musicals wishing I could sing, wishing that the world could only communicate in song, wishing I could be suspended forever in the anticipation of "Tonight."

Music

The Piano Recital

Watching child after child chop-stick their way through "Mississippi Hotdog," I wait for my five-year-old daughter's turn. Forty-five minutes into the program, her name is called. She slips out of her seat, the one where she couldn't sit still, and moves to the stage. She finds the footprints where the children have been told to stand for their bows, bends deeply, slightly loses her balance, but regains control to take her place on the piano bench. She begins. Her hands, having found the required notes, arch up and come down hard. As she plays her way through, she bites her lip. She is concentrating. She is determined. She has found that insistent rhythm, that heavy beat. She finishes, having remembered and struck every note. She starts down the steps from the stage, but with a gentle reminder from her piano teacher, returns to take her final bow. Her "Mississippi Hotdog" was, without any fatherly doubt, the best.

Our Song

You can't hear it without thinking of that meaningful moment, that moment when perhaps a hand touched a hand as the lyrics of some smooth love song slid inside you both to say what you both were thinking, or when perhaps you bought a CD together, brought it home, and found yourselves in each other's arms, or when perhaps you pulled each other close for that first slow dance, bodies flat against each other, soft whispers.

Jazz

I never have much liked it. I know I'm saying quite a bit about my musical sophistication by saying so. Oh, Dixieland jazz you might hear in Preservation Hall in New Orleans is fine, but that hard jazz that seems to slide notes onto their side is just too much for my ears. Instead, my ears seek the soft harmonies of the orchestra, the ballad, or the love song. So, when we were struggling to find our way through a major city in heavy traffic and I felt myself getting more and more nervous, I said, "Would you please turn that stuff off."

Coffee Houses

You can't find too many of them these days where a single performer, strumming a guitar under a pool of light, would sing of social justice. Once we believed that if we would just sing loud enough, if we would just learn the right words, and if we would just sing in harmony, we could fix the world.

Dance

Ballet Dancer

After being buried for three years
in my folder of newspaper clippings,
she stirs, ready for this frightened poem.
She looks hard over her right shoulder
as if pulled by a sudden noise or by words
she didn't want to hear. She turns
from any tale that tries to write her.
That long dark hair frames her narrow face.

The 22-year-old Boston Ballet dancer,
was thin, even for a ballerina, the paper reported.
But with each lift, she felt her own weight
as a yoke, a locked chain, a choking stone,
and when she danced for the mirrors,
they all said the same thing: Shed
more pounds. Shed more pounds.
Discipline, discipline, she told herself.

"It is not uncommon to tell a ballerina
to lose weight," the artistic director said.
"Dancers need a uniform body type. The art
demands it." And so she shed. And shed.
Everyone took note: First, she was applauded
for her efforts. Then, some asked if she was eating.
Then she was told: Do not lose any more.
But she saw herself as a work in progress,

A work that would end riding in a car
with her family on the way to Disneyland
because her heart could not maintain
the beat for a ballerina who was thin
as a swan's neck, who now backs
into the place where I keep her, bones
crossing bones, rattling the pages, always
insisting that there is work to be done.

Shadows

I loved watching her slow, careful movements behind the scrim, that female form, elevated, turning, the music coming to her like a warm breeze. She made the dancer's lines obey in that shadowed frame, made her body fold and curve before opening like a fountain, made those shadows into light. I sat in that dark theatre watching, mesmerized, until I heard a voice say what I wish I had never heard: "It's the beginning of a James Bond movie."

The Twist

There isn't much call for it these days, but I remember my teen years, gathering a crowd by turning, with just the right speed and elevation, my backside—back and forth, back and forth—to "Let's Do the Twist." I've felt its sweaty force. But since that happy moment, I've spent more of my life than I'd like to admit believing in the power of the Mamas and the Papas' version of "Twist and Shout."

Film

The Neighbor's Family Vacation

There's Jake getting out of the car at a rest stop. I just had to take some shots of those flowers. I've never seen a rest stop with so many flowers. Look at those chrysanthemums. Aren't they just beautiful? Now, here's the outside of Susan's house. It's small, but I think it's real cute. Susan was so happy because it had a fence for Muffin, but Muffin keeps digging her way out. She digs out and then just goes and lies on the driveway. Speaking of Muffin, here she is greeting us. And there's Susan—see how she cut her hair? I think it's sad she cut it. I like it best when it just sits on her shoulders. And that's me thinking I had the camera off—don't you like that shot of Susan's rug and my pretty feet? Now, here's Susan's living room. It's got lots of windows and lots of light. And her kitchen. When she gets a chance, she's going to get rid of those dark green walls. And here's the bath. Don't you just love those old-fashioned tubs? And her bedroom. There's Jake getting in the way of the camera. She doesn't have much closet space, but you never do with these old houses. Here's the other bedroom—that's where we stayed. Susan will use that room as a guest and catch-all room. There's Muffin's tail and there's Muffin's water bowl and food dish. Notice how I did that fade-out on that. Here's her yard with that big oak shade tree. That will help keep her cool in that Florida sun. What comes next is our day at Disney, but I'll just stop here.

No one suggested otherwise.

Fight Club

The premise that men might feel more alive if they would only beat the shit out of each other always struck me as rather silly. But a number of people whose opinions I respect said the film was worth seeing. So I went, and I sat there thinking that men who beat the shit out of each other in order to feel more alive are rather silly.

Thumbs Up or Down and One-to-Five Stars

Who can live under the whim of thumbs and stars; who can survive the force of that gesture or the clarity of that ink; who can let his or her life yield to their power?

In the Dark

Those six-foot faces, kissing, kiss you in that cool dark, let you climb inside. Those high speed chases, in and out of traffic, leave their debris behind as you drop your empty popcorn bag to the floor. Those bullets flying by, those knives slicing the air, those ropes around those necks push you against your chair away from the flickering light you can't stop watching.

Literature

Sharon Olds's "The Father"

I read poem after poem about connection, about how time is spent, about loss. I see her sitting there in his hospital room, watching him until he falls asleep, then slipping away into the waiting room for the breath to scribble those poems before he might wake again for his next meal. I see my father.

The Classics

They never go away. You hear them referenced in conversation with acquaintances that assume you know them. You see them in the bookstores when you're looking for something to read. You remember them being assigned in your English classes and your good intentions that never quite materialized. You even have some unread on your shelves at home. You keep thinking you'll make the time to read them. You want to read them or, perhaps more accurately, to have read them.

Sympathy Cards

There is always that section, away from the anniversaries, the birthdays, the graduations, and the holidays, that writes sorrow, usually in elegant print, beside a picture of flowers. On the cover, they always say such things as, "With Deepest Sympathy to Your Family" and "Thinking of You With Sincere Sympathy," and inside, a rhymed poem, like the following two from American Greetings:

> All of us are hoping
> That this message will reveal
> Our heartfelt understanding

Of the sorrow that you feel.
And you may find it comforting
At least in some small way
To know our thoughts
Are there with you
In sympathy today.

It's difficult at such a time
To know what words to say
But may God be with you always
To sustain you day by day.

Such poems convince us that it is indeed difficult "to know what words to say." Yet, surprisingly, such poems comfort.

This Piece

These entries show how art seeps into our lives, how it is with us every day, how we are always evaluating it, sometimes with the full force of moral obligation and sometimes with the ease of a passing eye. Nothing escapes. Having come to the end, I await my critics.

Justice

> *I advance a critical performative pedagogy that turns the ethnographic into the performative and the performative into the political. It is my hope that this pedagogy will allow us to dream our way into a militant democratic utopian space, a space where the color line disappears and justice for all is more than a dream.* (Denzin, 2003, p. xiii)

Justice is a social act, a way of being with others, of living that insists that we must keep care present in our actions and interactions, of moving through the world that requires us to treat all people with dignity and respect.

"In 2010, 1,277 children and youth under 18 years of age were victims of homicide."

U. S. Department of Justice, Office for Victims of Crime. (2012). *National crime victims' rights week resource guide.* Retrieved from ovc.ncjrs.gov/ncvrw2012/index.html

---

Justice, an obligation necessitating work in the social world, is a critical act, one that uncovers and marks the consequences of systems of power and privilege. Working for justice is critical if we are to be the people we hope to be.

Estimates of homelessness in U.S. range from 1.6 to 3.5 million people.

National Coalition for the Homeless. (July 2009). *How many people experience homelessness?* Retrieved from www.nationalhomeless.org/factsheets/How_Many.html

---

Justice calls upon the ethnographic. Based in the belief that understanding how others live takes us a step toward reflexivity and a step toward justice. Even in its most descriptive forms, ethnography carries a should.

"Number of hungry people in the world: 925 million hungry people in 2010."

World Hunger Education Service. (2012). *2012 World hunger and poverty facts and statistics.* Retrieved from www.worldhunger.org/.../world%20hunger%20facts%202002.htm

---

Justice is political, pitting those who wish to maintain the status quo against those who believe something must be done. The politics of justice is always an ethical question, always a question of where one should turn, always an issue that separates those who care from those who don't.

As of February 2, 2012, 4,800 U.S. soldiers were killed and 31,965 were wounded in the Iraq War, and 1,803 U.S. soldiers were killed and 9,971 were wounded in Afghanistan.

Washington Post Database of U.S. Service-Member Casualties. (2012). *U.S. war death statistics.* Retrieved from www.statisticbrain.com/u-s-war-death-statistics/

Justice finds its form in the performative, in doing, embodying, over and over again, ethical acts of turning one face toward another.

"In 2007, persons with disabilities were victims of about 47,000 rapes, 79,000 robberies, 114,000 aggravated assaults, and 476,000 simple assaults."

U. S. Department of Justice, Office for Victims of Crime. (2012). *National crime victims' rights week resource guide.* Retrieved from ovc.ncjrs.gov/ncvrw2012/index.html

---

Justice enacted is a pedagogical opportunity for us to see what might be done and an obligation to do more. Those who enact justice in their daily work offer a moral lesson, instructing us what it might mean to be a good student and teacher in the world.

"More than 34 million people now live with HIV/AIDS.

3.4 million of them are under the age of 15.

In 2011, an estimated 2.5 million people were newly infected with HIV.

Every day nearly 7,000 people contract HIV—nearly 300 every hour.

In 2011, 1.7 million people died from AIDS."

> amfAR, The Foundation for AIDS Research. (2012). *Statistics: Worldwide.* Retrieved from www.amfar.org/About_HIV...AIDS/...Stats/Statistics__Worldwide/

Justice is a utopian dream, unobtainable, but nevertheless an ongoing ambition, one that lets us keep moving forward (never quickly enough), and one that insists every inch forward is essential to the (exhausting) struggle.

"In 2009, 6,604 hate crime incidents were reported to the Federal Bureau of Investigation by local law enforcement agencies."

> U. S. Department of Justice, Office for Victims of Crime. (2012). *National crime victims' rights week resource guide.* Retrieved from ovc.ncjrs.gov/ncvrw2012/index.html

---

Justice moves forward through performance, a shared social activity that stages a better world for our consideration. Performance that reifies unjust structures and perpetuates oppression is nothing more than part of the problem. Performance worth doing and seeing reaches beyond itself, reaches into the possible and offers hope.

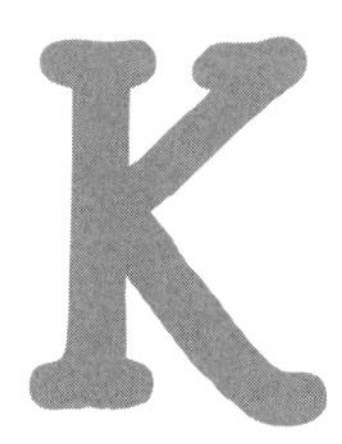

Knots

Waiting in the wing for the curtain to rise,
knots;
hoping the paint will dry before opening night,
knots;
struggling to find a line when ten lines have been jumped,
knots;
anticipating a laugh that doesn't come,
knots;
watching the futile effort to find a line,
knots;
seeing an old light board flicker on and off,
knots;
hearing perfunctory applause as the curtain falls,
knots;
knowing the show is a flop with four weeks to go,
knots;
listening to one's own crafted lines change as they fall from undisciplined lips,
knots;

Performance: An Alphabet of Performative Writing by Ronald J. Pelias, 125–127.

failing to find in rehearsal the words that might make a difference,
knots;
noticing a seam that does not hold,
knots;
agreeing, before reading, to stage an original work that doesn't work,
knots;
having only a few patrons in a house that seats hundreds,
knots;
sensing an increasing restlessness as the production proceeds,
knots;
reading a review that misses the point or crushes,
knots;
witnessing, sometimes for the better and sometimes not, what disturbs,
knots;
discovering that a needed prop is not in place,
knots;
approaching the audience or being approached when sitting in the dark,
knots;
complimenting, after all is said and done, when wanting more than anything to leave,
knots;
checking if what you've asked for will be done,
knots;
searching again for a design that satisfies,
knots;
pacing, wanting the lead's arrival,
knots;
realizing the next production depends upon the revenue from the one soon to run,
knots;

committing to a text, a part, or a line one doesn't understand,
knots;
believing that performance is your only true love,
knots;
losing lines you were sure you had,
knots;
investing in a single spectator's response,
knots;
knotting together all the what ifs,
knots.

Language

1

It's those words that deceive, that leave out more than they contain, that pretend to hold steady what quickly slips away; it's those canonical texts that come with such authority before they too are found lacking; it's those lines that speak directly to who we are before they begin to sound hollow; it's those arguments that motivate action before they fall away like empty promises: there is nothing secure, nothing to grasp, nothing to trust, only pretense pushes on, pushes us into our delusion that we have found an answer. Working with words is a fool's mission, a making of sand castles that will quickly wash away: consider how many words are launched with no discernable effect, how many carefully crafted words are designed to foster change but carry no power, how many wasted hours; consider, too, how words beget words, sometimes as fighting words, that sweep by without notice, how they are found and then forgotten, only to be presented at another time as something new, how they come with all their rules and regulations that keep some from being heard. This dictionary of false possibilities is nothing more than eggs cracking under the weight of elephants.

Performance: An Alphabet of Performative Writing by Ronald J. Pelias, 129–131.

2

Language comes to the mouth with promise,
        syllables of desire
                finding form
                finding sense
                        selected (with and without)
                                thought
discovers touching points,
        a reach beyond,
                beyond one body
                beyond denotative and connotative associations
                        into (for better or worse)
                                relationships
speaks the logic of the heart
        always a revealing snapshot
                even when trying to obscure
                even when diligently blurring
                        opening (connecting and disconnecting)
                                space
tells all it can tell
        a never ending imperative
                declaring yes and no
                interrogating the between, the maybe
                        an exclamatory (regardless of force)
                                interjection
performs its own form
        a tangled repetition
                looping back on itself
                knotting its knotted demands
                        until it strings together (delightful and disturbing)
                                surprises

3

They're all I have, these words I try to work. I am their director, discovering those I want center stage and those I want to wait in the wings. I guide them, nudge them along, trying to get the best out of them I can. I become frustrated when they don't act as I would wish. I work toward the vision I want them to enact. When difficulties arise, I try to find a compromise between my desire and what I can ask them to give. In the end, I must let them go. Sometimes they go their own way. Sometimes they write me. I am their designer, making choices from what is available to me. I select carefully, hoping that my decisions settle, find support with other decisions. I strive to have everything come together, form a picture that shows what needs to be shown. Work never stops until their curtain rises. Sometimes my designs never come together; sometimes they can't be read. I am their actor, letting them arise from within, letting them find their bodily shape. I long for the feel of them, the sense of them. I always want to be fully present, ready for how they might work me. I seek a blocking that lets them find their shape. I work them until I can claim them as mine. Sometimes they just push and pull me around. I am their audience, watching the work they do. I notice how they sound, how they emphasize this or that, how they come to me. I want them to move me, to make me feel I have spent my time well. Sometimes I like, perhaps too much, certain moments; sometimes, I am their worst critic. I am the words I work.

Manifesto

The continuation of performance studies as a field of study depends upon a strong commitment to the doing of aesthetic presentations. Without such commitment, it is a bankrupt discipline. Performance studies finds its heart in embodiment, in enactment. Only through staged performance, whether behind the proscenium arch or on the streets, does performance studies hold claim to a defining method, a method that understands performance to be a way of knowing. To use performance as a method, as is true for all methods, demands training. It requires practitioners to be fluent artists who know their way around the stage, who know what it means to call upon theatrical techniques as strategies of inquiry. This method of speaking from the body, like other forms of arts-based inquiry, brings forward understandings that are not found with objective, distanced methodological stances. Instead, the method of performance studies is an act of immersion, of becoming and being, of reflection and reflexivity. It tells what the body comes to learn.

To turn performance studies into a discipline that only occupies itself with studying performance in everyday and aesthetic frames from the position of the witness or with calling upon the metaphoric power of performance as an exploratory heuristic is a step toward disciplinary collapse. Others fields—cultural studies, English, philosophy, anthropology, to name just a few—do such work quite well, often with greater skill than performance studies scholars. What other fields do not do, however, is do performance.

Performance: An Alphabet of Performative Writing by Ronald J. Pelias, 133–140.

They do not present their insights on stage, nor do they believe that the aesthetic presentation of their ideas is appropriate or necessary to their arguments.

For the health of the discipline:

1. Performance studies artists/scholars must be trained in the use of the body as an exploratory tool for studying human communication and behavior. Performance studies artists/scholars must learn how to use the body as a site of inquiry, how to turn the body into a critical and reflexive posture, and how to speak from the body, both on stage and on paper.
2. Performance studies artists/scholars must make the doing of aesthetic performances central to their practice. Talking about performance has its value but is insufficient.
3. Performance studies artists/scholars must tackle in their performance work questions of significance to the human condition. Too often performances are offered purely for entertainment. They become a pleasant way to pass time and are soon forgotten. Performances must address what matters, make audiences feel, think, sweat.
4. Performance studies artists/scholars must work for presentations that create a better world. Performances that do not have an ethical reach should be cast aside as poor research and poor art.

Short of working in keeping with these four mandates, performance studies will become a forgotten practice that once upon a time could have made a difference.

Memory

Performance studies has long noted the ephemeral nature of stage presentations. In some instances, its ephemeral nature is framed as a lament since it troubles documentation and often does not translate into print scholarship, research that carries unquestioned academic legitimacy (for example, Espinola, 1977; Park-Fuller and Olsen, 1983; Taylor, 1987). As Espinola (1977) succinctly puts it, "performance lacks ... the stability of print" (p. 97). In other cases, it is marked as fundamental to performance's power. As Phelan (1993), for example, argues, "To the degree that performance attempts to enter the economy of reproduction it betrays and lessens the promise of its own ontology" (p. 146). In these next few pages, I write against the notion of vanishment by describing how three performances continue to live in my memory and by demonstrating how such remembrances influence my personal and artistic practices. Each of the three performances I isolate works in my memory differently; each is printed there, each teaching me about the power of performance and about myself.

I still see Nathan Stucky standing on the bare Kleinau stage. It was a faculty performance hour, and he had selected to perform an adaptation from Homer's *Iliad*, a section where Homer chronicles those killed in the Trojan War. The scene is primarily a listing of warriors who met their gruesome fate in battle. I had read the passage before and recognized how the scene functioned to establish rhetorically the horrific scope of the battle. It was a section I moved through quickly—the listing struck me as yet another depiction of the war's dreadfulness. Yet, with Stucky's performance I come to recognize much more.

Stucky makes me see each fallen warrior as a specific person, a person who was loved and whose body, violated by the technology of war, succumbed to a dreadful death. He does so, first, by playing on the genealogy that Homer provides. With each introduced combatant, Homer indicates the father/son lineage. Through subtle vocal work, Stucky reminds me of each father's loss, turning each fighter into a person whose life is valued, not as just another fallen soldier from the ranks, not as just another body in a weekly tally, but as a beloved son. He does so, second, through his own kinesthetic responses. Stucky, trained in the oral interpretation tradition, remembers well the standard lessons from the textbooks of sixties and seventies. Kinesthesis, as Bacon (1972) among the many from the time suggests, "is concerned with all movement that accompanies, reinforces, complements, and otherwise extends spoken language" (p. 11). I see Stucky's body suck in and tense as Meriones's spear strikes Adamas between the navel and the genitals. I witness Stucky's head tilt in grimacing pain as Aias's sword finds Kleoboulos's neck. I observe Stucky's body tighten as Meriones's arrow enters Harpalion's buttock and settles into his bladder. And in the seeing I am reminded of one body in sympathy with another, one body, Stucky's, feeling the pain and anguish of another's. Through Stucky's kinesthetic responses, I am told to remember. As I am told to remember, Stucky ends his performance with a projected picture of coffins, each draped in the American flag, from the Iraq war.

Stucky's performance is a lesson in craft. It triggers memories of techniques that were common in the repertoire of skilled performers during the era of oral interpretation. It encourages me to return "tone color" and "kinesthetic response" as essential vocabulary for training performers. It reminds me of the power, when done well, of oral interpretation's aesthetic. More importantly, Stucky's performance positions me, insists that I stop to consider the never-ending list of war dead from antiquity to present day. It shakes me from the numbness I've come to accept as a result of the media's daily barrage of war tragedies from around the world. It makes me pause, as Lockford (2008) does, before the listing of names she witnesses on Sunday morning television. It demands that I reject the easy slide into "just another." It requires that I attend as an empathic person, with humanity, with sensitivity to how lives matter. It penetrates, enters into my psyche, makes me remember, establishing itself, refusing to let go. It is archived, ready for and demanding use.

I met Lindsay Greer's work in performance, but it stays with me most forcefully as a text. I cite Greer's piece in its entirety—to do otherwise would seem an injustice:

> A rabbit hopped across Jen's lawn. It was a baby, a little ball of fur. She said she felt such love for it, like a mother, that she wanted to put its head in her mouth. Not to bite it, but just to have it there, its fur on her tongue. Its warm little body, shaking, breathing, afraid and loved.
>
> Joe said that when he desires someone, he can feel it in his jaw. When he sees a man he wants, his jaw begins to ache. He has to move it so it won't go numb. As the pain in his jaw increases, his desire grows so fierce it becomes unbearable. He must win the man or lose his teeth.
>
> I listen for the way my own body desires. My jaw doesn't ache, but I feel it in my teeth. If I were all teeth, I would eat him into nothing but bone. I want to bite his chest, as if trying to eat out his heart, but I don't want him to die. I want to hold him in my teeth, take him into my mouth, my throat, and inside. I feel hungry. This makes sense now, why I always tried to control hunger. This is why I would stuff the desire down and watch as it rose again, leaving my body unsatisfied. How silly. You can't control what your body asks for. You can't silence the hum of your longing. Put its head in your mouth; shaking, breathing. Shaking, breathing, afraid and loved.

When I first met this piece, Greer was an MFA student in Cinema and Photography, a person I didn't know well who took my Writing as Performance class. Beyond the introductory pleasantries, my first extended conversation with Greer was about this text, a text she wanted to know if she should perform for class. She read it in a quiet voice in my office.

"Wow," I said, when she finished. "May I see it?" I wanted to hold it in my hands. She offered me her typed page with some hesitation.

"Do you think it's okay?" she ventured.

"I think it's wonderful. I love how you write desire—so raw, so direct, such startling images. And the sexual puns are just delightful. 'Eat him into nothing but bone' is just too good. How you flirt with the surreal is so compelling. It just takes my breath away. And the return in the last line of 'Shaking, breathing, afraid and loved' from the first paragraph captures so well the interplay of desiring and desired. Wow."

Greer's text, still etched in my mind long after first hearing it, establishes for me the strength of Graver's (1997) typology of corporeal presences. I meet the *character* in Greer's piece, the interior and exterior of a fictive presence who invites my contemplation. I am taken in by the *performer* who displays technical proficiency, an expressive body that understands how to write. I see the *commentator* who knows how women's desire has been rendered and who refuses conventional restraints. I read her text as further evidence in an emerging sense of her *personage,* built on my limited personal history with her and the stories about her I've heard. I see her as a *group representative* who is marked as a woman and who speaks from a socio-historical position. I am led to her *flesh,* to the body that stands as a physical entity, made of skin, hair, muscle, blood. I sense a body of *sensation,* one attuned to its possibilities and demands. Graver's scheme tells me what is in play as I witness Greer share her text. But the body that most commands my attention is one Graver strategically avoids—the real person that gives presence to these other bodies. Graver, rightly so, omits from his topology the "real" person. He does not wish to posit a "foundational reality" (p. 227); instead, he sees each body as "a way of representing oneself or, rather, a way of representing oneself within a particular discursive domain" (p. 227). Yet, despite knowing better, I cannot keep from asking: Is Greer's text just a playful, literary excursion or is this how she really feels?

This question haunts, insisting that I ponder why I want to know the answer. Is it that I am simply participating in the typical male fantasy of insatiable female desire? It is that Greer's text taps into my instinctual, animalistic nature that social decorum has so carefully taken away? Is it that I recognize my own sense of desire in Greer's writing and want the comfort of resonance? Is it that I desire to be the object of desire, hungered for, to have what has been missing? Is it that I wish to live in the fullness of desire that Greer's text articulates, that I long for carnivorous consumption, one body taking in another? Is it that I believe life without deep desire is empty, barren, pointless? Each of these narrative possibilities is, of course, true, or, to adapt Graver's language, each is "a way of representing myself," but none offers a sufficient explanation. What I do know is that Greer's text stirs my own personal psychology, adamantly requiring my ongoing attention. Her text will not let go.

As I am sure he does for many scholars in performance, Dwight Conquergood lives in my memory. He will always be archived there as a vibrant example of what it means to do performance studies scholarship with passionate commitment, dialogic engagement, and ethical responsibility. When I think of Dwight, and I often do, much comes to mind—his compelling critical ethnographic studies, his persuasive voice as a disciplinary advocate, his precisely crafted essays that have given us an abundance of discipline defining vocabulary, his keen and sensitive presence, his gentleness. Such remembrances are always accompanied with a performance I had the privilege of seeing Dwight do on several occasions. It was a performance of a street gang oath of allegiance, a statement of loyalty to the group. Although I have lost much of the content of the actual pledge, the memory of his performance comes forward with a specific gesture: Dwight's closed fist pounding his heart. This gesture was done with such vigor I worried that Dwight was putting himself at risk, that his heart could not withstand the blows. But, of course, Dwight's signature was to put himself at risk, to carry more than one could expect any heart to carry.

Dwight's gesture, a gesture I trust mirrors the ritualistic performance of the oath, functions for me as an icon, a performative moment that symbolically holds more than can be articulated. It points back to the street gang in a display of their cultural commitment and solidarity, an allegiance so deep that their hearts are pounded into presence, given to the group, bestowed in the name of membership. I believe Dwight would be pleased with this reading—he would want my attention to be drawn to the street gang, to see its members as cultural participants who have their own way of making sense of the world, a way guided by their own cultural expectations and ethical dictates. Yet, I am also drawn to Dwight, the performer, who selects this performance moment to stage, and, in so doing, demonstrates how a single gesture can collect meaning, can assemble an array of themes, can carry the significance and heart of a piece. Dwight's choice reminds me as a teacher of performance that the artist has the capacity to capture in a single behavior a phenomenological essence, an action so telling that its description cannot account for its power or its resonant truth.

I also feel Dwight's gesture pointing at me, accusingly. Dwight, the exemplar of doing critical ethnography right, demonstrates the full potential in Bacon's (1976) call for a "sense of the other," a charge Dwight frequently cited. He shows me what engaged commitment is, how one might stand with others, profoundly, ethically, compassionately; how one might enter into worlds not one's own and leave with an expanded sensibility, leave as a better person; how one might embrace those who through circumstances, politics, or prejudices are less fortunate, might meet the moral imperative to place oneself in a position of participatory care; how one might live what one preaches. Dwight's work tells me that I have preached from the safety of the performance studies pulpit, but have failed to enact its promise. My efforts have not even touched the outer limits of Dwight's compelling circle. As I move toward the end of my career, I am saddened and made weary as well as hopeful and joyous by Dwight's example. Available in my memory's archive is Dwight's encyclopedic body of work located in a gesture, ready to be pondered, pored over, preserved—Available as an ethical guide.

Having performed my memory of these three performances, I must acknowledge that memory is personal, idiosyncratic, and often distorted. I apologize to the three performers I've discussed for the unfortunate ways in which my memory might have unhappily bent their work. I've tried to bring them forward in ways that they are all still alive for me, still printed in memory. My defense rests with writer Jane Hirshfield's (2007) suggestion: "Art lives in what it awakens in us" (p. 28). My archival record contains nothing more than what continues to be of use, both as a teacher of performance and as a person. My memory holds the ephemeral in place, insisting on space, a stage for future performances. It invests in the stock market of ideas and passions, capitalizing on my needs, inadequacies, and ignorance.

Naming

In my dream, the play was written by Edward Albee, who claimed he thought it was his best work, much better than *Who's Afraid of Virginia Woolf*, but no one would recognize it as an Albee piece. Directed by Lee Breuer and designed by the collaborative efforts of Paul Brown and Bunny Christie, the play was an environmental masterpiece in constant motion. Robert De Niro, who just wanted to be a part of the production, agreed to work the curtain. As the curtain rose, Jesse Eisenberg and James Franco entered, crossing the stage holding hands. They stopped center stage, looked at the audience, and walked off. Cuba Gooding Jr. was then dropped from the rafters wearing only a pair of sunglasses which led to a quick scene between Helen Hunt and Jeremy Irons about propriety on stage before Angelina Jolie appeared with all her children who were reprimanded by James Earl Jones for their rowdiness. Kevin Kline was laughing up-stage-right while Nicole Kidman began singing her ABC's down-stage-left. A brief film, difficult to make out but clear enough to know that Shia LaBeouf and Jane Lynch were rowing against a stream in a small canoe, was shown while John Malkovich gave a speech about the difficulty of finding one's identity. During Malkovich's lines, Jack Nicholson's voice could be heard off-stage, saying "I've got mine. I've got mine, baby." At that point, Sir Lawrence Olivier offered acting lessons to all the actors who had previously appeared. Mary-Louise Parker and Sarah Jessica Parker, appearing behind a scrim, wondered

Performance: An Alphabet of Performative Writing by Ronald J. Pelias,141–142.

why they had three names and why people often confused the two of them while Anthony Quinn, Lynne Redgrave, and Jean Stapleton did a Greek dance with much more flexibility than one would have thought possible. Meryl Streep came out and took a bow and the applause lasted at least twenty minutes. Spencer Tracy was flirting with Kathleen Turner, but the audience, cued by a flashing sign, booed until they left the stage. Peter Ustinov, coming on with great flourish, insisted "The only reason I made a commercial for American Express was to pay for my American Express bill." Jon Voight started crying, but Mae West told him, "Buck up or fuck up." "X" failed to show-up, and You, sitting front-row-center, were disappointed, but all was redeemed when, in a completely satisfying deus ex machina, Rene Zellweger, playing the role of Zorro, flew across the stage just before I woke up.

Opening

Performance is an opening, a location—a curtain drawn, a wooden floor washed with light, a window that invites the voyeur, a circle in the square, a podium that stands before, an arena of play, passion, and purpose. It is an opening where ghosts find form, linger, and haunt. It is an opening where eyes, with and without their consent, look. It is an opening where we find ourselves. Here, words slip into the cracks.

Performance is an opening, a transitional, liminal space, where one learns, for better or worse, the heart of the social, the clash of the cultural, and the twist of the linguistic. After, one may never be the same.

Performance is an opening, a grave, a place where one moves from life to death. There is always mourning in what cannot be held. There may be some joy in what can be remembered.

Performance is an opening for the ego, a place where self shouts me. It happens when there is too great a need to be seen, to take a turn, to say I matter. It happens when performance becomes nothing more than a competence display, when performance is nothing more than a seduction strategy. It happens when performance fills with arrogance, thinks it deserves the time it takes.

Performance is an opening, a grand or unremarkable event, noticed by few and missed by most. Its choir always sings its praises and needs its nourishment. Its distracters always want something else. For them, it is a corrupt church not worth attending. They drive by without a thought.

Performance: An Alphabet of Performative Writing by Ronald J. Pelias, 143–145.

Performance is an opening, a slice in the side, a wound. It is the opening that deals with how the body bleeds, that tells a tale until wound turns into scar. It allows each injury to be considered, felt. It may heal or harm.

Performance is an opening, a breach, a deconstruction of the discursive system, be it artistic, linguistic, or social, that offers possibilities. Some of the possibilities are available for reflection; some imply needed action. Some frighten, cause us to retreat. Some promise hope; some not. Some are right; some are wrong.

Performance is an opening, a conversational turn, punctuated in the ongoing flow of discourse. It never knows its beginning or end, although it often assumes it does—curtain up, curtain down. Its end is always carried into other beginning.

Performance is an opening, a vacancy, a job to be filled by the willing. It calls, demands a presence, demands labor. It pays on its own terms.

Performance is an opening, opinion's opportunity, a pandering to and policing for the powers that be or a proposing of an alternative position or prodding into action. It is an opportunity to pause and ponder, to point and profess, to preach and pardon, to promise and please, to push and perfect, to puzzle and prove, to praise and preserve, to process and provoke. It is an opportunity to paint the future. It is an opportunity to pose, to pass, to project oneself into another and to possess, to purify, and to produce oneself. Performance is plentiful.

Originality

The one adequate measure: History.

Pledge

I am driven to write, driven by those (for example, Hantzis, 1998; Buzard, 2003; Madison, 2006) who fear that the performance of personal narratives comes at the expense of the Other. I write pledging my allegiance to my ongoing process of navel-gazing. My commitment to navel-gazing finds its seduction in the fact that my navel so quickly leads me to the Other. In this recuperative gesture for navel-gazing, I first offer a series of personal narratives that become present for me when I take the time to ponder my center. I then address the question of why I continue staging personal narratives, why I persist in going where my navel leads me when I gaze upon it.

Gazing At My Navel

When I gaze at my navel, I see an oblong indentation, perhaps an inch long, in the center of my abdomen. The sides slide into its deepest parts and its middle puffs up like a swelling boil. When my fingers pull back its surrounding skin for a better view, two small, unconnected scars appear, slightly darker in color. Its appearance is strikingly present for view. Overall, it is not attractive. But that was not always the case. Years before my belly grew into a ripe melon, my navel was mysterious, deep. Its secrets were hidden; its bottom was not to be found. That was the time when my navel collected lint as if it wanted a blanket. Like tentacles, the hairs around my navel would reach out and gather cotton fibers to make my navel's covering. "Let's see how much you made today," my partner from that era would say,

Performance: An Alphabet of Performative Writing by Ronald J. Pelias, 147–155.

and we would lift my shirt to expose a round ball of fuzz. "We could make a pillow if we saved each day's bounty," she once commented, but we never acted upon her promising idea.

I miss the playful intimacy we once had, the comfort of one body with another as my shirt would lift. There was no embarrassment, no self-conscious hiding, no sense of risk. Simply, together, we would marvel at my navel's work. It became a site for teasing, a shared comedy, a moment of closeness. My navel's labor gave us pleasure in a relationship that we were too young to make last. My navel leads me back to her. She returns, teaching me about relationships, about the joys of shared intimacies, about one body learning and relaxing into another.

When I gaze at my navel, I remember that the first hands that touched my body clipped my skin and knotted a reminder of my connection to another, to my mother. Cleaned and wrapped, I was placed in her arms, arms that have held me for all of my years. Trying to recall the stories of my birth, I called her. "Mom, I'm writing a paper about navel-gazing, and I'm hoping you can help me," I tell her.

"About your navel?"

"Yeah, about navel-gazing—you know the expression, don't you?"

"Are you going to write about how your navel collected fuzz?" she teases.

"I might," I say, having forgotten that my mother knew about my navel's ability. "What I really wanted to ask you," I continue, "was about my birth, about how when I was born I messed up your ability to have any more children."

"You didn't do that," she responds. "You're confusing your story with your Uncle Gene's. When Bobbi had Gene, the doctors just ripped him out and Bobbi couldn't have any more children."

"Really?" I question. I've heard all my life that I was the reason we had to adopt my sister, that I had done damage with my entry into the world.

"That's right. You're just confused," she says. I do not think that I am the one who is confused, but I decide to let her have the story of her present telling.

"So I shouldn't feel guilty, then?" I reply.

"No, honey, you shouldn't feel guilty."

"Well, I'm glad I don't have to carry that any longer," I laugh.

"No, you don't," she says, laughing, too.

Whether my memory or hers is correct, I do not know for sure. Perhaps, if I accept her version I will lose part of the love that locates itself in the psychology of remorse, in the pain of knowing you hurt someone you love. I do not, however, trust that bit of amateur psychologizing. What I do know for sure is that I love archiving the navel's family connections with my mother. Such a practice helps me remember how blood can flow uninterrupted, how the nutrients we need pass from body to body, how skin finds its meaning in skin.

In this process of archiving family, of contemplating my navel, I find myself with my sister. "Do you remember, when you were little, Gus [my brother] and I told you we were going to unscrew your belly button and your bottom would fall off," I once asked her. "Of course, I remember," she laughs, "I was petrified." I find myself with my father, my first golf coach. "The proper position for the five iron," he taught me, "is straight from your navel." Before his death, when the home nurse would come to give him his bath, he would say playfully, as he struggled out of his clothes, "Don't tickle my belly button today." And I find myself with my brother, teasing my elderly mother: "You're not too old. You should get your navel pierced."

When I gaze at my navel, I am brought to the erotic, to that small center midway between, to that crevice of secrets, fetishized by some. I remember my daughter, budding into sexuality, wearing women's fashions cut to put her navel on display. I remember her, after my futile attempts to persuade her otherwise, coming home from college with silver rings hooked through her young skin. With her pierced ears, nose, and belly, she was decorated, ready. And I remember others, those who welcomed the finger's gentle circles or the tongue's wet entry. Once, a friend told me he knew a woman that if he touched her navel just the right way, he could bring her to orgasm. I was skeptical but intrigued by our bodies' possibilities. I think of those whose navel is no more alive than elbow skin, eliciting no more response than a nudge on a crowded subway. And I recall those who recoil at any approach. "Why does everybody want to do that?" she said, tensing, stopping me from traveling to that forbidden place. I have learned that the navel is a space, like other body parts, of interpersonal sensitivity, negotiated publicly and privately. It hides, flaunts, and yawns as others approach.

When I gaze at my navel, I see the frivolous, comic, and gross uses the navel has had to endure. There is Sergio Garcia's spitball shot, landing a bit short of his target on the belly of a supermodel who, with a slight flexing of her tanned and toned muscles, rolls Sergio's shot in, all in the name of selling beer. There is the champagne, spilled into the navel's cup, ready for the drunken party-goer insisting upon a sip. There is my college roommate's finger, placed inside his navel, each time he is about to fart. And there are the boys, pushing in the sides of their belly buttons, to imitate the anatomy of their opposite sex.

When I gaze at my navel, I return to Vietnam, to the soldiers who cradle their guts, blown open by enemy fire, who groan waiting to be put back together. Some would add to the body count of their generation; some would be patched and scarred. My job was to assist the doctors as they went about their attempts at remaking. One doctor, observing his finished work, remarked, "He no longer has a navel." I imagine this doctor startled from sleep, images of missing body parts circling his head. I envision this soldier, after being nursed back into physical health, wondering if the woman he is falling for would turn away if he took off his shirt. And I see the woman he is falling for, understanding, her fingers lightly tracing the scar where once his navel was.

"What are you working on?" my partner asks.

"I'm writing a piece about navel-gazing," I answer.

In a flash she is online. "Here's Graham Barker's 'The Incredible World of Navel Fluff.' It says he has 'the world's biggest collection of one person's navel fluff (lint), as certified by Guinness World Records,'" she reports. "Oh, yuck," she blurts out as she scrolls down. I am pulled by her exclamation from my desk to see what has garnered such a response. Three large jars of lint, marked 1984–1993, 1994–2000, and 2001–, fill the screen. Each jar contains different colored lint, perhaps a result of time or changes in Graham Baker's attire. The first specimens are a dab brownish grey, the second a sour faded pink, and the third a bluish dark grey with a sprinkling of the faded pink.

"That is gross," I say, staring at the image. Her fingers quickly move across the keyboard and we are in YouTube, viewing singing navels with eyes and nose drawn above. There are the faces, wiggling with the belly's weight, the navel an open mouth. There are the comics, making their navels talk and sing. Some are funny, some not, but what surprises is that each video seems to me a bit pornographic. I'm invited into a bizarre intimacy with a mediated body I'll only ever know by the few inches above and below its center. After we witness five or six singing navels, they all begin to seem the same, and we switch to piercings. We look at the decorative displays, but a needle pushed deeply into the center of the navel, a seemingly masochistic act, stops our browsing. "Enough," I say. "I'm trying to write where my navel leads me."

"It led you here," she replies and shuts down.

Telling Navel Stories

I pledge my allegiance to navel-gazing because navel stories are telling. They tell of my connection to others, some with whom I enjoy a close relationship, some to whom I am a stranger. With the first group, I function as an insider, an ethnographer who uses his privileged position to uncover the familiar, to understand what a given experience might say about the human condition. With the second group, I strive, with all the ethnographic sensibility I can muster, to enter into another way of being. In both cases, my navel stories position me in relationship to others.

I pledge my allegiance to navel-gazing because all gazing, those kept private or those publicly shared, are social acts. To keep silent, to refuse to tell what one carries inside, is to acknowledge that all people are socially situated. Silence lives in awareness of consequences. I may not share because of shame or embarrassment, because of a sense of propriety, or because of an ethical responsibility to others, but each time I choose not to speak, I do so because I am thinking of the other. And when I tell the most intimate details of my life, I do so always aware that all my personal feelings are located interpersonally. To be personal is to be with others.

I pledge my allegiance to navel-gazing because I believe in the power of the single individual who speaks from the position of the "I" and who is willing to share what he or she understands as true. Only then can I fully tap into that vibrant and exhilarating complexity that constitutes human life. Only then am I given the fullest opportunity to stand by another empathically, without assumptions, without belief that my empathic response could ever be more than a partial understanding. Only then can I drop my illusions of superiority, my ethnocentrism, my arrogance.

I pledge my allegiance to navel-gazing because I trust the case study, my own and others', to provide a view of the individual who is situated within an historical and cultural context and who is draped with every utterance in ideology. Such studies, with their reflexive turns, put on display a socially constituted self, a self that has the potential for change.

I pledge my allegiance to navel-gazing because my white skin is a reminder of my privilege, a reminder of how in so many ways I am privileged and of how I carry a social responsibility to work for social justice. I support navel-gazing because I see individuals who do so function as witnesses, as social agents, as interventionists, as the creators of alternative ways of being. I see when reading those who look inward an ongoing obligation for myself to all those with whom I share this planet. I see the work it accomplishes and the work ahead.

I pledge my allegiance to navel-gazing because I value all bids for being. My stories, your stories, generated from the center of our being, are interjections, interruptions, and interventions in the ongoing conversation of everyday life. Our tales are a way of taking our turn. And we deserve a turn, not because we are self-absorbed, but because we live amongst others, working to make sense of our world, striving to have meaningful connections with others, and insisting on our right and responsibility to be relationally and politically present in the conversation.

Power

1

Having power, critics eat what they want. They set the table to their own liking and then gorge themselves on what others have cooked. They dominate the dinner conversation.

Having power, critics muscle in. They flex and pose, wanting all to admire just how hard they are. Their definition is set, sculptured by the repetition of their daily routine.

Having power, critics take center stage, wait for all eyes before delivering their monologue. They live in anticipation of applause.

Having power, critics carry their comments like tokens to be tossed to the needy. They can spot the hungry with a glance. They thrive on others' starvation.

Having power, critics babble on and on. They exhaust what might have been appreciated, might have been seen for what it was, might have been taken in.

Having power, critics ask nothing. Answers slide from their mouths like snakes.

Having power, critics stand above it all to decide what will do. Perched on high, their comments land like bricks.

Having power, critics come, under the light of their own star, as wise men who think they have gifts. More often than not, they unwrap their own presents.

Having power, critics hoist their flag and insist that everyone march to the anthem they want to sing.

Having power, critics trump whatever else has been played. They hold all the tricks. They try to remove all the jokers from the deck.

Having power, critics cut up and cut down whoever displeases. They are knives ready to dissect, to slice. They carve their own image.

Having power, critics move like a heavy boot that heels the ant.

Having power, critics are fire to straw, wind to leaf, rain to snow.

2

Once there was a little girl who drew a picture of a pumpkin pie. She liked it very much but she wasn't sure if it was very good. She showed it to her parents. They said they liked it, but she worried that they liked it just because she was their daughter. She showed it to her friends and they said they liked it, but she wondered if they liked it just because they were her friends. So she decided she would ask the critic.

She had heard that the critic was a wise man who knew about such things. She had to wait a long time before she could see him. When her time finally came, she showed him her picture. He told her that it needed this and it needed that. She brought it home and worked on what he had said. She returned to the critic and he said that she shouldn't do this and she shouldn't do that. She worked some more and then returned again. He started to say that he "would almost be able to taste it if she would" when she reached down and pulled the pie right out from her picture. He saw her holding it in her hands. Then, without much of a stir, he said, "If you turn it just a bit, it might catch the right light."

3

When critics point to what they think is wrong, they censor. The censor's first word is "Don't."

Don't do that.
Don't include this.
Don't keep that.
Don't leave this.
Don't go there.
Don't.

When critics point to what they think is wrong, they have their reasons. They know what is good and in knowing, they censor.

Do that.
Include this.
Keep that.
Leave this.
Go there.
Do as I say.

When critics point to what they think is wrong, they censor on behalf of their own legacy.

Do that, in my name.

Include this, in my name.

Keep that, in my name.

Leave this, in my name.

Go there, in my name.

Do as I say, for me.

Quality

"A culture of criticism thrives on finding fault with every person, every argument, and every thing (including itself)."

(Goodall, 2000, p. 28)

Unable to escape
measures of good and bad
hands that lift and drop
yardsticks of permutations and iterations,
unable to stop
naming and pointing,
parceling out, privileging,
eliminating,
I take my turn.

Performance: An Alphabet of Performative Writing by Ronald J. Pelias, 157–161.

"... criticism is as inevitable as breathing..."

(Eliot, 1932/1964, p. 3)

Stamped legitimate and approved
by guards at the gate,
by dissertation and publication,
by the race through the ranks, the awards,
I pontificate,
swollen with the accumulation of years,
with all the authority of the slot I fill
with all the authority I allow myself
to believe I've earned.

> *"Critics are people licensed to express their pleasure, their desire, their values in public judgments of art, and they are licensed to do so not only because they are knowledgeable technicians but because their personal take on the world and on art is deemed useful by those who are not critics."*
>
> (Steiner, 1995, p. 60)

My use comes by carving,
shaping a body to fit
a tradition, a method, a belief,
marking differences, gradients
by applauding, by saying no,
separating the remarkable from the pedestrian.
Armed, I mold and form.
I sever, slice, and slash,
cutting until it appears.

"Criticism is like dissecting a dead frog.... They're examining all the guts and shit and organs, when the thing that really matters, whatever it was that animated the body, has long since left. It does nothing for art."

(Wilson, 2011, p. 202)

Scalpel on flesh,
knifing my way in and out,
I fear more than stitches
the deep, destructive wound,
the heart
damaged by my probing hands.
The whole critical procedure
stops the pulse.

"What is this itch
to invoke valuation, to seek out verdicts?
The critic, the bureaucrat, the insecure
all crave a pointer with which to cause rupture."

(Dobyns, 1996, p. 84)

I too have been there,
exposed,
the critic coming too close
calculating, closing in,
me, backing against the wall,
arms crossed,
jumping with each jab,
wanting to listen, learn, be liked
and I've found myself lacking.
I've felt their words inside:
snake eggs hatching.

"It's not easy to stand psychologically naked, undefended and unrepentant, before an audience of intellectuals, many of whom get more pleasure out of criticizing than admiring."
(Webb, 2011, pp. 39–40)

I've been held by delicate hands,
coddled, when I deserved dismissal,
wrapped in welcoming arms,
comforted, when I failed.
Pathetic, needing kindness, lies,
I've been embraced.
Having fallen on my face,
I swallow the pain
with a smile.
A maggot
under the branches
of a swaying fruit tree.

"I must insist how disturbing this is—
the necessity
of going public, of being a fool."
(Dunn, 1994, p. 256)

As critic, as performer,
I resist the summons,
the necessity
of words
that push and pull,
of hands
that stroke and slap,
of eyes
that watch and twitch
in the name of art.

"Goodbye rhythm, goodbye rhyme
Talk to you another time.
When you get past the capacity to react
What you get to
Is the end of the line."

(Clark, 1984, p. 78)

Criticism is a matter of standing
on the rusty razor's edge.
Quality is knowing
when the razor's edge
cuts into your feet.

Reflexivity

1

Everything Pelias says might reduce to the claim that performance is hard so we should be nicer to each other. Sorry, sometimes criticism just cannot be nice. Sometimes the truth hurts. Often, lies are more hurtful. Performers need to know when their art falls short. Students need to know when their work is inadequate. And we all must be able recognize our own shortcomings.

2

Pelias keeps arguing that researchers must capture the emotional dimensions of any phenomenon under investigation and keeps trying to write poetically in the hope that readers will get some feel for the events he describes. I must admit that I was never moved by any of the book's entries, and I think that is the book's greatest flaw. The writing is never quite up to the task he has set out for it.

3

All the whining and whining—writing about performance is hard. Most readers probably start in agreement but by the end are saying, "Just buck up. Things aren't as bad as you say." Or maybe they are saying, "Try laughing at yourself and all of us who struggle from day to day to make sense of our lives and our work."

Performance: An Alphabet of Performative Writing by Ronald J. Pelias, 163–167.

4

After reading the entire manuscript I'm not sure what new knowledge I've gained about performance. The book fails to demonstrate how it is in dialogue with ongoing work. While I can appreciate a clever phrase here and there, I don't know what the book ultimately wants to say.

5

Why Pelias thinks readers would care about his thoughts about performance is beyond me. His ideas, like most people's, are rather ordinary.

So what would we have if we took Pelias's advice to write from the heart? I think his offerings give us all the proof we need: We would have article after article sharing personal feelings but article after article without substance.

6

Every entry makes essentially the same point. While the subject may change, each one stands as an argument for a kind of scholarship. After a while, it just becomes tiresome.

7

It's hard to see how all the pieces are performative writing. As a result, readers never quite know what they are reading.

8

It would have been nice if Pelias had elected to write about just one well known performance. The few actual performances he describes have had limited visibility, so in many ways the question of whether performative writing can capture the spirit of a theatrical production remains unanswered.

9

The book loses a sense of its own privilege. It is so marked by white, middle class, heterosexual male perspective and bias that it becomes difficult for anyone of another positionality to read through the whole thing. It often asks for identification, but you have to start at a place that is close to the author to begin with if that is going to happen.

10

Pelias really is too close to his book to see it for what it is—a small effort that will have little import for the field. His rhetorical task, over and over, is to make himself look clever. Sorry, he isn't, once you see what he is up to. I find it a rather pathetic display.

11

Pelias is trying to undercut critical response by including this entry, but the strategy is too obvious to achieve its aim. Quite simply, this piece suggests only a few of the ways the book falls short.

12

Pelias's book changed my life. I'll never think about performance the same way again. I'll never offer critical commentary the same way again. I'll never approach my own performances the same way again. I'll never be the same again.

Rehearsal

A gathering seeing them all, seeing them together taking in feeling the tension, the promise the jittery and the comfortable moving into a tight circle a joke, some nervous laughter a call to attention a vision, a concept reading stop watch on the table list of tomorrow's tasks

Finding characters back stories, true stories, script stories relationships, moving toward or moving away alliances, attractions resistances, repugnancies a contextualizing clock a location's comfort and discomfort beginning point, end point and the actions in between defining words, discussing lines a meaning set, formed the mind's instruction

Finding characters bodily experiments a hand, a posture, a tilt of the head a tone, a quality, an attitude the movement of motives the sound of desire found, felt, figured somatic possibilities intuitive affirmations agreements to be assembled the body's requirements a place to go

Blocking one body alone one body next to another arranged into a picture a portrait that tells allies and adversaries the center, the background, the ready the space, thin or thick, between speakers and listeners a fourth wall honored or broken entrances, exits touch, planned and purposeful organic, determined staged reality or dream

Parts of the whole bits and pieces a scene, a moment focused, intense labor again again again improvisations, finding the bones, locating the heart details again, try again a sound, a curve, a saying from trial and error to tried and true again toward the set, the yes until the body knows

Lines, lines, lines learn them patience frustration speed through lines, lines, lines patience dead space, deadlines words matter, syntax matters, order matters lines calls from the stage, calls that rob the rhythm, sink the scene insistence patience until claimed, owned

Reminders not on that line, but the next energy project concentrate down right, not center energy position the chair place the cup remember have fun at 7:00 tomorrow

Inhabiting claiming space a set to use the step down, the swing of the door, the slide of the sofa costumes to wear the tug of the shirt, the noise of the shoes, the rub of the ribbon props to hold the weight of the whip, the size of the stamp, the scarf pulled from the purse living there possessed, owned

Late changes: that's just not working cut that line instead of sitting there, come behind try this bit additions and subtractions a quick scramble testing the limits of what can and cannot be pushed anxious moments

Tech the necessary interruption ladders, wrenches, gels missed cues lighter, darker up a level a slower fade the light that marks shades colors focuses an atmosphere, a mood, a feel another statement

Emergencies: death in family, gone; illness, gone; censored, gone air conditioning, quit; light board, quit; costumer, quit no sales, no show panic scramble resolved

Opening night energy anxiety audience, eyes ready to look anticipation a curtain conceals, then reveals lights actors' fingerprints, signatures watching the watchers applause, perhaps polite, perhaps pounding degrees of satisfaction congratulatory comments some accurate, some not

Closing night a final chance a sigh a celebratory funeral a rehearsal for the next production.

S

Seduction

Performance seduces me, pulls me in, makes me want to hear. Its seduction comes in many resonant and dissonant forms, forms that enter me, that tell me who I am and who I'm not. I welcome all the resonant and dissonant voices as a potential impetus, as a possible case, ensuring my return. I proceed by revealing why I continue to place myself in the presence of performance, why I spend countless nights directing and witnessing bodies on stage, why I want to hear others' resonant and dissonant voices, why I welcome the seduction.

Seductions

I am seduced when I feel that stirring, perhaps in the form of a faint fluttering, or a creeping tension, or a heavy weight deep within, or a slight dizziness, or a desperate attentiveness, or a hard swallow, or some other disturbance in the calm of my anticipation. It's the jolt, the reminder of my own and others' humanity, in all its joys, sorrows, and pains. It's the capacity, the willingness to enter that space, to see how words write on bodies. It's the body refusing to be still, the heart refusing to stop, the tear and the fist refusing to be held back. It's those moments that tell me I care.

I am seduced when I am pushed beyond myself, put in a new place where I can see what I couldn't before, put in place by the error of my former thinking, put on an alternative path. Seduced, I must put two and two together, must put up or shut up, must put an end to where I was. There is no putting off, putting down, or putting away that which must be put forward.

Performance: An Alphabet of Performative Writing by Ronald J. Pelias, 169–177.

I am seduced when I find myself in the presence of right-minded people, people like me, people whose sense of the world is the same as mine. We join together in the comfort of our wisdom and sing in the choir of own making. And when our time together is done, we leave feeling stronger, feeling confident we can now encounter those others who are not right-minded with greater compassion or with greater fury.

I am seduced when I am caught, implicated by words that seem to slap me across the face, that shake me from my smugness, that point me out as naïve, as insensitive, as hypocritical. And since I do not like to see myself as naïve, insensitive, hypocritical, I try to change so that I might once again return to being one of the right-minded people, might once again return to my smugness.

I am seduced when I am moved to action, made to understand what must be done, forced to see how the plight of others cannot be ignored. I am most likely to take action when I feel most deeply, when I empathize, when I am brought into another's painful world. I never carry Brecht's worry: my caring is never left at the theatre door; my caring carries me forward.

I am seduced when language licks its lips before the kiss, when language slides beyond its skin, when language tongues its way down my spine. Or, if that seems a bit overdrawn: I am seduced when language insists that I stop, that I consider how it is working its way in and around me, that it is marking what I hadn't seen marked before. Seduced by language, I linger, slip into its curves, its curiosities, its call.

I am seduced by skill, by the articulate, by the ability of one body to stand in for another. Craft, carefully hidden, cradles me, allows me to rest, to settle as if I am in cupped hands. I am collected, captured by competence, taken in, but unaware until after the fact that technique claimed me. It is the seemingly unplanned planned, the unwanted wanted, the unnoticed noticed. It holds art's heart.

I am seduced by its "live-ness," its "now-ness," its potential for failure, for death. I go to see it live, in that moment, in that space, in defiance of its premature demise. I go to see it reach its end, its final bow. I applaud its life-lived, relish that I witnessed its survival from curtain to curtain. I feel it as an accomplishment.

I am seduced by its space, set for viewing, before it all begins. Pulled into its promise, I anticipate how space will become a meaningful place, a place where objects will come to matter, will be touched, handled with indifference and care, a place where behavior is shaped, changed, a place where I might or might not want to enter.

I am seduced by the event, by bodies gathering, finding their way in, looking, seeing who is there, seeing if they are seen, settling in, hearing the rumble, the murmurs, the laugh that leaps out, sensing when to move to silence, to straight-ahead attention, and then, at the end, after the applause, by bodies leaving, finding their way out, seeking the world beyond the stage, watching their step, processing what they had just felt, offering thoughts, sometimes with exuberance, sometimes quietly, and after some time, putting the shared darkness behind them.

I am seduced by performers, the attractive ones, the witty ones, the bright ones, the odd ones, the crazy ones, the outlandish ones, the intense ones, the genuine ones, the believable ones, the ones who sing and dance, the ones who seem to be enjoying what they are doing, the ones who reach beyond the stage, the ones who seem to be speaking just to me. In short, I am seduced by all the ones who keep me from separating them from their roles.

I am seduced by history, the work that washes me into another time, that warns from the past, that wears the present moment. I am seduced, too, by the history-making, by what revises, by what stands in contrast to what has come before. History seduces me because it is art's anchor, its aesthetic guide.

I am seduced by repeated encounters with an actor across roles, with the ability of an actor to be more than herself or himself. As a single body locates its different shapes, I marvel at what one actor can do, what one actor can become. I celebrate difference, how it distinguishes, how it measures.

I am seduced by what disturbs, by what I can't reconcile, by what I can't understand. Thrown into the puzzle of it all, I try to make the pieces fit. When I can't, it haunts, troubling me. It alarms and compels. When I can place it into clear focus, its possibilities diminish. Clarity couples too easily with closure.

I am seduced by the drama—the escalating tensions, the heightened energies, the high stakes—and by the resolutions—the considerable consequences, the winners and losers, the cost. I want to believe that interactions matter, that words spoken carry weight, that actions have importance. I want to believe in the lessons that unfold before me. I want to believe I'm learning how to live.

I am seduced by the lights that direct my focus, telling me when and where to look. The beams that mark space, that create mood, that come in different hues to let me see what I must and slip into the shadows, into the in-between. They illuminate through the dark.

I am seduced by a directorial hand that shapes, stamps a vision, an absence and presence, that uses the stage to speak. I welcome the theoretical claim, the political message, the metaphoric signature forged on the bodies of actors. I welcome the artists who are not afraid to put themselves forward, who are not scared to take a stance, who are not troubled by tradition. I welcome the artists who understand art as a form of expression.

But most of all, I am seduced by the freedom to look, to sit back in the dark and to consider, with all that my head and heart will allow. Given a gazing license, I am the voyeur who takes it all in, takes what others offer, takes until satiated. My applause tells the degree of my satisfaction.

Sexuality

On stage, I like it
straight and simple,
easy to read
the ingénue, young and supple,
standing there, singing
to her handsome love
and he, a smile dancing on his face,
takes her hand and waltzes
into the perfect duet.

I like it all
mixed up, hard
to figure, confusing
as a surreal dream,
keeping me guessing,
wondering how desire might play,
how bodies might find their place
between and around
what I thought I knew.

I like it flirtatious,
establishing the drama
of the possible, of the maybe,
the tension building
with a touch here and a touch there,
a glance that lingers,
and those smiles that say
you know what I'm thinking,
you know what I want.

I like it complicated, watching
how people make sense of it all,
how they turn desire
into so much more than biology,
so much more than a needed release,
how they find their way
with others, by way of the head
and the body, by actions,
by words surrounding yes and no.

I like it subtle, restrained,
a cockatoo's call without the cock
titillating without the tit,
no flaunting, no exposed flesh,
parading like a beast in heat,
no strutting, no blatant show
of the crude and coarse,
inconspicuous,
a whisper in an ear.

I like it poked,
laughed at, parodied,
lampooning all that wondering,
all that earnestness,
all that chasing, that energy,
all those bodily contortions
with accompanying grunts and groans,
all that coming together
as a testament to love.

I like it intimate, a quiet
lesson on how to be
in another's arms,

how to take in and be taken
by talk, by the slow seduction
sex earns, a safe place
of sharing—a breathing in,
a giving, revealing the truth
that words and touch can carry.

Stink

"I'm sorry," he said to the woman on the plane. "I believe that is my seat next to yours. I'm afraid you'll be the unfortunate person who has to sit next to someone who stinks. I should say I didn't always stink," he said taking his seat. "Stinking came on me about two years ago, and I can't seem to shake it. You see, I was an actor, and I had the good fortune or misfortune to get several roles, one right after the other. The only problem was that by all accounts I was just terrible. The other actors and the director were initially patient, but I knew they were growing increasingly unhappy with what I was doing. I just never could get it right. My friends were kind, but I could tell their supportive words were hollow. The critics, of course, were brutal. Even in shows that seemed to work fairly well, I was marked as the exception, the person who kept the show from being what it might have been. Now, in an actor's career, one might survive after one or two poor performances, but after getting all those roles, one after another, and doing so poorly, I became synonymous with bad performance. People started comparing my work to other bad performances. It wasn't long after that I became a benchmark for how bad a performance could be. People would say, 'Well, at least it wasn't as dreadful as a Spenser' or 'that stunk as much as a Spenser.' Once your name becomes definitional, it settles in, grabs hold of you.

It's a part of me now. I bathe at least once a day, sometimes two or three times. I've tried every deodorant they carry, even tried baking soda and bacterial disinfectant. But I still stink. I step out of the shower, I stink. I scrub my arm pits, I stink. Nothing works. Some days are not as bad as others, but I always have it. It usually smells like a mix between some chemical pollutant and a dead animal. I'm not sure what animal, but it's pretty far along. Maybe for your nose it registers a bit differently, but the chemical and dead animal notes are definitely there, and, like I said, it's been with me for about two years.

I was in Paris when I first noticed it. I needed to get away, away from all the talk, but there was no escape. The most romantic city in world and there I was, stinking. At first I thought it was from some chicken I ate—it didn't seem right when I shoved it down—but I didn't get sick or anything. I've gone to doctors, and they confirm that I stink, but they don't have an explanation or a cure. So I live with it as I'm afraid you must until we reach our destination. I wish I didn't have to impose on you.

My wife lasted about six months before she couldn't take it anymore. I don't blame her. At first she was sympathetic. She tried to help, but then the winter months came and it was harder for me to stay outdoors. We started sleeping in separate beds, and that helped for a while, but the smell soon permeated the house. You couldn't sit anywhere without picking up the smell. I think if the roles were reversed, I would have left, too. I do miss her. After all those years together who would have thought this is how it would end. I miss our friends, too. Like with most divorces, friends have to pick, and you can't blame them for picking her rather than Mr. Stinkpot here. Even our dog, Rascal, picked her. Whenever I went into the room, he would put his paws over his nose and give a little whimper. You'd think people, not to mention my dog, might get use to it, but I haven't found anybody who can handle it for long. I really can't stand it myself. So, I am truly sorry," he said again, noticing that her eyes were wide open, round as saucers, her head was slumped down, tilted toward her shoulder, and her mouth was agape, a steady drool dripping down her chin.

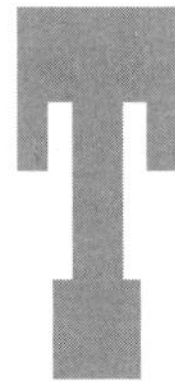

Taking

1

Take it in like medicine, knowing it's good for you, knowing it will make you better, knowing it will fix you. After all, those in the medical arts wouldn't prescribe what they didn't think was needed. Inoculations are for your own protection. Surely you don't want to be diseased.

Take it in like a medical instrument that probes, here and there, searching for what is wrong. Just try to relax. The procedure will be over shortly. No need to be tense. No need to worry. Just wait until the results are in. Soon, there will be a diagnosis.

Take it in like the skin greets the scalpel, resistant but yielding to the sharpness. The wound will only be as deep as the heart. Don't be concerned. You'll be anesthetized and cauterized. Infection is unlikely.

Take it in like a feeding tube, slowly, intermittently gagging. Welcome that smooth snake knowing it is your only way to survive. Feel yourself fill by what is put in. Soon you will feel bloated. Eliminate what you cannot process.

2

Take it in like you are driving a car on ice. Creak along when you hear the ice crack. By your snail's pace, stay on the road. Look left and right to see danger's edge. If you go into a skid, release your foot from the gas. Don't hit the brake. Turn into it.

Performance: An Alphabet of Performative Writing by Ronald J. Pelias, 179–181.

Take it in like a deep breath. Feel yourself expand. Exchange the old for the new. It is a process you can never stop. To do so would be sure death, death by desperate refusal.

Take it in like your favorite food. Chew on it until its juices slip from the edge of your mouth. Let it sit on your tongue before swallowing. Gorge yourself until you can't take another bite. Forget the fact that at the end you may still be starving.

Take it in like an old lover's touch, without worry, without effort, as the mind falls into the body, still, calmed by the familiar hands, hands that now rest softly on your chest or slowly stroke your arm until you decide, against sweet comfort, that you must get back to work.

Truth

To capture the truth in performance—the truth that reaches beyond an easy equivalency or simple correspondence to the world, the truth that pulls audiences into the theatre, the truth that gives credence to the claim that performance has the potential to change our lives—enact the following steps:

Step 1

Since the truth in performance is a matter of knowing what truth to tell, live with your script until you find its pulse. Follow its veins to its heart. Feel it beat, over and over again. Feel it beat its way into you. Feel it beat until you know its rhythm, its sound, its song. Reject familiar tunes, tired melodies, predictable orchestration. Do not speak until you can speak from within its heart. Do not let its arteries carry you away. Do not forget what matters. Then, you may be flirting with the truth.

Step 2

Since the truth in performance reveals itself through concealment, finds itself from what it buries, use your craft to figure the fortunate lie, to fix your passionate presence into form. When your invisible scaffolding settles into place, when your calculated choices turn into the insistent and the invisible, when you forget what is no longer foreign, you may be forging a truth, naming the notable.

Step 3

Since the truth in performance lives in the body, is recognizable and felt, let your body lead, listen to its claims, linger in its call. Sink into its somatic summons, its sensuous seduction. Slip inside instinct; be ready for response. Know that your body may lie. Be careful. When your body is alive and alert, when it inhabits a relaxed tension, when it speaks without your direction, when you believe you can trust it, you may be moving forward as a possibility.

Step 4

Discard the steps.

Ubiquitous

Before entering Panera, I stop to blow my nose (Performance of Personal Maintenance). I believe some might object to such a display of bodily functions in an area for dining (Performance of Respect). My wife, Mimi, waits until I'm finished (Performance of Patience). Once inside, Mimi and I fall in line to wait our turn to order (Performance of Civility). We read the menu posted on the wall above the cash registers (Performance of Capability), sometimes moving a bit out of line to make the words on the wall come into clearer focus. We signal we know our place (Performance of Politeness). As we approach the register, we greet one of the Panera servers who has taken our order many times before: "Hi, Cole. How are you doing?" (Performance of Friendliness).

Cole smiles and starts ringing up our usual request. "I'm great," he says. "Let's see. We need one French toast bagel with honey walnut cream cheese and a large ice tea to go with that, and we need one blueberry bagel with regular cream cheese and a coffee in a to-go cup. Both bagels sliced and toasted. Right?" (Performance of Competence).

"You got it," my wife says (Performance of Approval).

"You're the best, Cole," I add (Performance of Appreciation).

We gather our food and containers for our drinks and find a booth for two. We place our coats on our seats and our food on the table (Performance of Territoriality) before going to get our drinks. At the coffee station, a man, oblivious to the fact that several people are waiting, is blocking the entire space as he fixes his own cup of

Performance: An Alphabet of Performative Writing by Ronald J. Pelias, 183–185.

coffee (Performance of Self-Centeredness). Those of us waiting look at one another with facial expressions that seem to say, "Some people" (Performanceof Disapproval). The man finishes his task, turns around and sees we have been waiting, but says or does nothing to apologize (Performance of Rudeness). I return to the table and share with Mimi my negative narrative of the man's behavior (Performance of Superiority). I stir my coffee and then take a sip. I pull the napkin to my lips for a quick pat (Performance of Consumption).

As I cover my bagel with cream cheese, I notice a man sitting at another table talking with a woman whose back is facing me (Performance of Watching). The man, who is eating a pastry and talking without a pause, resembles the image of Jesus that is found in European mythology (Performance of Culture). "Look," I say to Mimi, "Jesus decided to eat at Panera today" (Performance of Play). She turns her head to get a glimpse and then rolls her eyes at me (Performance of Resistance). "Don't you think he looks like Jesus?" I push.

"Yes, a Western Jesus," she replies, a bit exasperated (Performance of Displeasure).

I am about to let my conversational direction die when I notice a bald man who has more pounds on him than his doctor would advise sitting alone at a table by the back window. "Not only is Jesus eating in Panera, so is Buddha," I say, amused with myself (Performance of Access). Mimi's eyes roll again, but I sit there wondering what Jesus and Buddha might say to each other if they were sharing a meal at Panera (Performance of Imagination).

Our conversation changes to matters more mundane. "Do you want to stop at Kroger's on the way home?" Mimi asks. "I was thinking about making chicken pot pies for dinner and I need to pick up some cream and there are a couple of other things I think we need" (Performance of Planning).

"Sure, pot pies sound great," I say (Performance of Consent).

"Let's also stop at Rural King and get some more bird feed. We're almost out," Mimi suggests.

"Okay. While we are there, we can also see if they have those Christmas lights we want," I add (Performance of Agenda Building).

As we are planning for our day's tasks, Sally and Sam, a

couple we've come to know because of our frequent visits to Panera, appear at our table. "Hello, you two," Sally says in her cheery voice (Performance of Familiarity). "Mimi, I wanted to show you the pictures of the purses I made. I sold three of them at the Cedarhurst craft fair," she says poking at her iPhone to make the pictures appear (Performance of Display). "That's one I sold," she notes with a big smile (Performance of Pride). Picture after picture flashes before Mimi's eyes, each with a description of how it differs from the others (Performance of Documentation). Mimi smiles and nods, inserting an occasional "lovely" (Performance of Generosity). Sam catches my eye: "These women can go on and on about such things." I shake my head in agreement (Performance of Masculinity).

"Come on, Sally," Sam says, taking hold of her arm. "Let's give these people some peace" (Performance of Impatience).

"I hope I didn't bother you with all my pictures," Sally says, looking to Mimi (Performance of Inquiry).

"Oh no. They were fun to see," Mimi replies (Performance of Kindness). We exchange goodbyes and part with smiles (Performance of Sociality). Mimi and I deposit our empty plates and drinks in the waiting trash containers (Performance of Appropriate Customer Behavior). We make our exit as I reach for my handkerchief once again (Performance of Repetition).

I write this brief account (Performance of the Obvious) in which performance is reduced to doing (Performance of the Everyday).

V

Vulnerable

Performance "is a profound engagement with a vulnerable self. It is an act of being nakedly human, publicly." (Roloff, 1973, p. 3)

Returning to this quote, I still feel the risks of performance deep in my bones, perhaps more so now than when I first encountered it in the beginning of my teaching career. Over the years, I've often shared this quote with my introductory performance classes, usually as an admonition that students who offer critical remarks to performances should do so with care. I want them to recognize the harm they can do. I want them to know that I understand what I'm asking of those first-time performers. I want them to know how we should behave.

Returning to this quote, I see those vulnerable selves, one after another, take the stage, unsure of their beginning efforts. They are unsure of the rules, unsure of the possibilities, unsure of each other and of me. They hold their scripts until the very last moment. They fix their clothes and arrange their poorly chosen props. They begin and then ask to begin again. They call for lines. They feel the eyes watching. They feel naked, subject to public humiliation and shame. Calling the next name on the list can, at times, feel cruel.

Returning to this quote, I remember how I have always felt vulnerable on stage, exposed, wanting more than life itself to be done; how I never could move beyond self-consciousness, hearing myself speak and watching myself move, as if I were an object, one to be mocked, ridiculed, and dismissed; how I could not stop my hands and

Performance: An Alphabet of Performative Writing by Ronald J. Pelias, 187–189.

legs from shaking, could not keep my voice from quivering, could not remember my lines; how, when finished, I wanted to escape, separate myself from what had happened, never see those who were present ever again. Performance always comes with the implicit assumption that one merits a turn. I have never felt that confident.

Returning to this quote, I think of the various texts that ask more of actors than they may feel comfortable giving. Vulgarity, blasphemy, nudity, misogyny, racism, homophobia, all those things we write off with the explanation that it's just a role, one that serves within the context of the script an ethic that actors should support. We make such arguments and then claim that by playing different roles actors might develop compassion for the characters they enact, might learn alternative perspectives, might change their lives. Actors become in some measure the person we ask them to be.

Returning to this quote, I reach for all the performances of personal narratives I've seen. They come to me as examples of how the vulnerable links to identity, often telling the tale of those who have been oppressed and who will no longer be silent. In such a public stripping, courage triumphs over fear. Such work stages an ethic for consideration, points to power, and positions us around a should. And after the performance is done, after the theatre door has been locked, such performers on the way to their cars glance nervously over their shoulders.

Returning to this quote, I am reminded of those acting methods designed to help performers to stand before audiences in all their nakedness, designed to shred pretence for the sake of the real, designed in the pursuit of the honest and of those directors who keep asking for more. Give, they say. Giving is how you'll receive, they add. The choice to stand in front of audiences vulnerably, to allow oneself to share with strangers what many people find difficult to share in their most intimate relationships, to be nakedly human is to believe that such displays link us deeply to our core. It becomes art's difficult and glorious reward.

Returning to this quote, I imagine performers on stage, standing together, depending upon each other, willing to trust in each other. Cues will come. Entrances will be made. Props will be left. And if the unimaginable should occur, they will be there, ready to help. A foundational faith, earned in rehearsal, will keep all in place, will hold vulnerability in check.

Returning to this quote, I get a glimpse of myself sitting with the audience, in darkened space, unaware that I have placed myself at risk. I take in what is before me. I am only dully aware of how it might position me, poison me. As I watch, I may realize that my thinking is suspect, may feel disturbed, may sense that I'm being accused. I may think I am in control, but I may discover that I am not, may find that I am changed. As an audience member, I am vulnerable to the power of what is before me.

Returning to this quote, I return to my first teacher of performance, Lee Roloff, who taught me the pleasures of watching and being watched and the necessity of being open, vulnerable, to others.

Watching

Performance is nothing more than an opportunity to look, unencumbered. By paying close attention to each other, we learn what it means to be human and what it means to exist. Without looking and being looked at, we lose a sense of ourselves (Woodruff, 2008). The marked space of performance is designed for the eye. Stare all you want. It's yours for the taking.

Performance is nothing more than a story bidding for our attention. It's like any consumer product; it survives only when enough people buy it. To make theatre work requires good marketing, good advertising, and, in the end, people who want to purchase again and again what is on display. In a capitalist culture, sales matter. Look at the bottom line.

Performance is nothing more than a mimetic, representational reminder. In this looking glass, we see the best and worst of ourselves. The mirror, often to our surprise, may distort or even shatter, making it more or less difficult for us to see (Abrams, 1953; Turner, 1982; Conquergood, 2002). Mirror, mirror, on the stage, who do you think we are?

Performance is nothing more than an ideological statement, more often than not reinforcing cultural norms. It often boasts of its ability to change world circumstances, but its typical fare does little in that regard. It's a luxury for the privileged, made, for the most part, by the elite for the elite to keep the elite in place (Eagleton, 1990). See yourself dancing on stage with those just like you.

Performance: An Alphabet of Performative Writing by Ronald J. Pelias, 191–195.

Performance is nothing more than a struggle for visibility, an opportunity to insist on presence, to demand notice, to show oneself. It creates a time when one can take a turn (Munoz, 1999). It often fulfills both a personal psychological need and a political necessity. Step forward so we can see.

Performance is nothing more than a text to be read, a semiotic code whose signs may be as easy to comprehend as a beginning reader or as difficult as a scholarly treatise in a forgotten language (Bennett, 1990; Carlson, 1990). See what you can take in. Notice the signifiers and signified. Watch everything slip away.

Performance is nothing more than testimony, offered by one or more eyewitnesses who give their words. Their intent is to say nothing but the truth (Felman and Laub, 1992; Zingaro, 2009). We sit in the jury watching the proceedings, deciding what and whom to believe.

Performance is nothing more than mere entertainment. It's a pleasurable way to pass a few hours, to get a few laughs or hear a few songs, and to see the trials and tribulations of life without having to suffer the consequences. For the price of a ticket, we can be mindless, free from the obligation to remember. Sit back, relax. No one will disturb us in this air conditioned space. Enjoy. See what you want to see.

Performance is nothing more than a theft from life on behalf of the fictional. It claims its thievery shows us more than we might otherwise see. Robbing the real for the possible, it insists that spectators speculate on the likelihood of it all (Dolan, 2005). Given hypotheses for consideration, we watch for what might appear, for what might become the new truth.

Performance is nothing more than an act, a doing in keeping with other doings, a presentational and discursive fit. Such repetitive behaviors are often unremarkable, but can, when turned at just the right angle, allow for alternative actions, for alternative viewings (Butler, 1990, 1993). Be alert for the slant. Sometimes, it is hard to see it coming.

Performance is nothing more than identity on parade. We applaud the beautiful and vilify the ugly. We feature the privileged and turn the unworthy into functionaries and villains. We create the space that reflects us and wonder why we sit alone. Once again, there we are. Do you see us moving across the stage?

Performance is nothing more than the transformation of the chaos of our lives into a digestible form (Langer, 1953). It shapes experience into the knowable, into a sense-making narrative that makes us, at least for a moment, believe in meaning (Eakin, 1999). As we sit there looking, our lives become figured.

Performance is nothing more than what culture uses as performance. Every culture determines what constitutes performance and what performance is worthy of seeing. Every culture puts performance to its own use, deploys performance for its own interests (Schechner, 1993). It's all controlled, predetermined. Notice how performance struggles to be seen in cultural cracks. That, too, is part of culture's use of performance.

Performance is nothing more than strategized coercion, a controlled manipulation designed to bully us into the logic of its making. Through carefully chosen behaviors, we are pulled along, turned this way and that, until we are strong-armed by its crafty power (Kershaw, 1999). Watch yourself watching. See how you feel.

Performance is nothing more than a metaphor that connects our lives to how we go about the business of living (Burke, 1945). Understanding performance as fakery turns humans into an unlikeable lot. It's depressing. Thinking of performance as doing establishes humans as active agents who create, for better or worse, their world. We like to believe that we can spot the genuine.

Performance is nothing more than articulated choice, offered at the expense of all other available choices. In this violent act of selection (Bogart, 2001), decisions are made for our viewing. We take in what is there, often missing what has fallen away. Vision has its price.

Performance is nothing more than an ethnographic claim. Based on cultural study, performances reveal what has always been and what might be (Madison, 2005; Spry, 2011). Such cultural work allows us to assess how we have gone about the business of participating and observing, how we do and do not fit in. Seeing how our lives compare, we can consider change.

Performance is nothing more than an invitation for empathic engagement. Opening ourselves, taking imaginative leaps, and struggling to enter other worlds are the basic requirements (Pineau, 2011). As we do so, lives unfold before us. We can choose to push away or to pull in. See what we gain by taking in. See what we lose.

Performance is nothing more than method, a succession of set and evolving procedures designed for inquiry (Pineau, 1995; Pelias, 2008). Like any good research tool, it uncovers what was previously hidden. Above all else, it demands participatory practice. Imagine moving toward the stage and taking a role. See yourself using your body as a means of exploration. What did you discover?

Performance is nothing more than materialized memory, set for viewing. By giving consent to an enactment, a construction of past life experiences becomes fixed, established for the future. It becomes the story that tells. Remember, we are nothing more than what we can see.

Performance is nothing more than and nothing less than art. It crafts its observations for our observational pleasure. Its desire is to satisfy our desire. Reaching for the tear, the laugh, and the outrage, it works the affective to solicit our affective response. It puts into action the action it wants us to take. It locates itself in a history of aesthetic demands, knowing that we are demanding. We come to watch.

Writing

Q: When did you start working with performative writing?

A: Once I realized that criticism ignores the heart of performance.

Q: How would you define performative writing?

A: A pear beside an apple tree anticipating its own rot.

Q: In your mind, is it a performance on the page?

A: It's a series of entrances and exits with a few moments in between.

Q: Does the poetic have a place with performative writing?

A: It serves as performative writing's aesthetic company.

Q: How is the "I" situated in performative writing?

A: At language's mercy, scrambling to satisfy desire.

Q: What does reflexivity offer the performative writer?

A: A specimen, pinned and squirming on the wall.

Q: Does this imply that performative writing is an embodied practice?

A: The body longs for and struggles to escape the pin.

Q: Performative writing, then, is material, has consequences?

A: Ideas do not matter when severed from the body.

Q: What are you hoping to accomplish with this book?

A: To produce a reader I like.

Q: I find many inconsistencies in your book in regard to your views on performance. Intentional?

A: Different rooms offer different pleasures.

Q: Why use the alphabet when performative writing seems to be an escape from representation?

A: Structures hold our lies in place.

Q: Do you have a favorite entry?

A: Time locates favorites, tells what broth might splash from the soup.

X

Xenophobia

When did it begin
With a single head shaking a disapproving no
With someone mumbling, "That's not right," from a dark auditorium
With a public slap from some critic writing for the *New York Times*
With troubling laughter from a dwindling vaudeville audience
With a social consciousness?

When did we decide
You are too foreign, too strange, for me to know
You have a way of being I could never understand
Your everything is just too different from my everything
You are just too far over there and I am here
You do yours and I'll do mine?

When did we come to believe in an ethic
That trumps our method, that limits sensuous embodiment?
When did we turn away so that we wouldn't offend?
When did we come to accept that performing others
Was nothing more than an act of colonization, of exploitation,
Rather than an empathic reach?

Performance: An Alphabet of Performative Writing by Ronald J. Pelias, 197–198.

When did those scholarly arguments give us pause?
When did we start being so cautious
That looking at anything but a mirror seemed wrong?
When did we draw lines around difference?
When did we begin to guard our space
While others guarded theirs?

When did we learn to be afraid?
Are we better off now, now that we've walked away?
Are we the people we want to be?
Are we missing what we once had?
When did we tell ourselves that we are doing enough
When we just do ourselves?

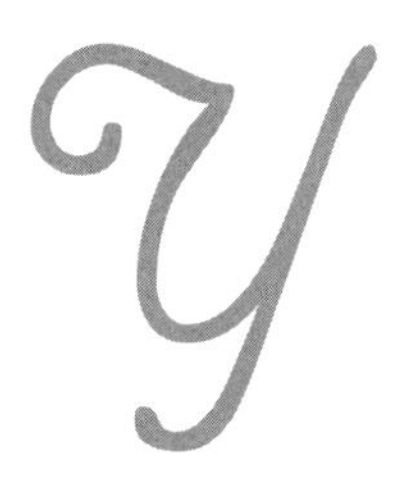

Yearning

CHARACTERS

Professor Larry Stone (Theatre faculty member)
Crystal Hunt (undergraduate theatre major, junior)

SETTING: The cluttered office of a theatre faculty member, filled with memorabilia from previously staged productions.

AT RISE: Professor Stone is sitting across his desk from Crystal.

PROFESSOR STONE

If you were my daughter, I'd tell you to change majors. Find some other field that will give you some security. Forget about theatre. It's a cruel profession.

CRYSTAL

I can't do that. I love what I do.

PROFESSOR STONE

You sound like so many students who have come through this office. They all profess their love for theatre, but find, once they leave here, that their lives are just one disappointment after another.

Performance: An Alphabet of Performative Writing by Ronald J. Pelias, 199–203.

CRYSTAL

I know the odds are against becoming a big star and all, but I can't give up on my dream.

PROFESSOR STONE

Your dream is most likely to turn into a nightmare.

CRYSTAL

Why are you saying this to me? Do you think I'm not talented enough?

PROFESSOR STONE

You are talented, but talented doesn't mean much. There are so many talented people out there who are trying to follow their dream. Talent, I'm afraid, has very little to do with success. Or happiness. All I'm saying is that if you want to be happy, find another profession.

CRYSTAL

I can't believe you are saying this to me. You're a theatre teacher. You're supposed to support your students.

PROFESSOR STONE

I'm just being honest with you. Would you rather I paint you a big old lie?

CRYSTAL

I'd rather you be supportive. We all know it's tough out there.

PROFESSOR STONE

Let me tell you my story. I was just like you. Grew up doing theatre. Loved being on stage. Decided to major in theatre. Even in my first years, I was getting good parts. By the end of undergraduate work, I was the departmental "star." I landed very major role that came along. I could sing, dance, and act—a triple threat, as they say. Won all the awards you could win. Because I was involved with someone, I made the decision to stay in the program for my MFA instead of heading straight to New York for what I was sure would be a fulfilling acting career. The MFA only gave me more confidence, and soon after finishing the MFA, I was off to the Big Apple. I spent ten years there, and some would say I had a successful career. At first it was hard to find work, but by the end of my time there I was making a living doing commercials, some voice-over work, getting some television and some off-off- and off-Broadway parts here and there, a few traveling shows. Then, one day I woke up and realized that my life was empty. The work I was doing I could do in my sleep. Nothing was challenging. My "art" was nothing more than a commercial enterprise, something that anyone, with just a little training, could be plugged in to do. That's when I decided to try teaching.

CRYSTAL

And is teaching as empty for you as your New York years?

PROFESSOR STONE

Perhaps one day you'll know what it means to teach twenty-year-olds to play Willy Loman.

CRYSTAL

They also get to play Biff and Happy.

PROFESSOR STONE

And you got to play Linda, Willy's suffering wife.

CRYSTAL

I think I learned quite a bit from playing that role. I learned what it means to be with someone whose dreams fall flat.

PROFESSOR STONE

Ah! The liberal arts justification for theatre.

CRYSTAL

You taught that to us.

PROFESSOR STONE

Yes, I did.

CRYSTAL

If you don't mind me saying so, I think you're sounding like Willy Loman.

PROFESSOR STONE

That's my point. A career in theatre is likely to turn anyone into Willy.

CRYSTAL

When Linda can't cry at the end of the play it's in part because she is angry with Willy for taking away their dreams. When she finally breaks down, it's because she accepts their dreams are lost.

PROFESSOR STONE

Biff has it right. Willy "had the wrong dreams. All, all, wrong."

CRYSTAL

Willy was a salesman, Charley says, and "A salesman is got to dream." So is anyone who loves the arts.

PROFESSOR STONE

Those who love the arts have the wrong dreams.

CRYSTAL

Those without dreams are left in tears.

PROFESSOR STONE

We've trained you well.

CRYSTAL

What do you mean?

PROFESSOR STONE

You've become a salesperson. A salesperson for theatre.

CRYSTAL

I've become who I allow myself to dream.

PROFESSOR STONE

And who have I become?

CRYSTAL

You get to decide. You can be Willy Loman or you can be someone else, someone who takes some satisfaction in what you've done.

PROFESSOR STONE

And what have I done?

CRYSTAL

You've lived your life in theatre. That's a dream come true.

PROFESSOR STONE

Is that enough?

CRYSTAL

Yes, that's enough.

PROFESSOR STONE

Are you sure?

CRYSTAL

I think so.

Z

Zeitgeist

Resolution, that plotted cliché, exchanged
For endless links, broken lines, and fragmentary leaps

The well-made play is the well-wrought
Urn shattered into pieces

The curtain is to the stage
As the pause is to the pedestrian

Performance cracks against the real
A purple egg in a bird cage

The voice and body, trained
An ideological sweep, a political crime

The mirror reflects the quotation
The quotation, twisted, the intervention

The body's technological extension
Another eye, another ear, another arm, an other

Marching into the normative
To undo its doings

Performance: An Alphabet of Performative Writing by Ronald J. Pelias, 205–206.

The aesthetic for the everyday
The aesthetic in the everyday

Spectacle reaches for filmic effects
The juggler drops the fifth ball

Transitioning beyond binaries, places
Of never-ending never-endings

Being gives way to becoming
Reality turns into relationalities

Translational accuracy to postmodern play
Potentialities and possibilities, unanchored

Moving the personal into the political
Walking on a bed of broken glass

What's in the world for
What's good for the world

Individual psychology, motive to
Cultural systems, discursive practices, power

The communicative desire, connection
A loose thread

Identity, prey for capitalist exploitation
A longing for the obligation of the shared

History's future—always the next big thing
Its past—always what once was the next big thing

Since the beginning, a gathering
To witness and to assess

Addendum

I had the vision of ending this book with some type of summary note. I thought that I might write one more poem, one that called attention once again to the alphabet structure. I even started to play with a few lines:

> **A** is for what appeared
> **B** is for what sits hidden below
> **C** is for what you caught
> **D** is for what you dropped
> **E** is for what you entered
> **F** is for what you forgot
> **G** is for …

As you probably agree, it was a good idea to abandon this closure. This poetic attempt felt forced—too many "for what's" and too many "is's" for its own good—and even more, I think we can agree we've had enough of the alphabet by now. Also, I was beginning to dread finding something that might work for "X" and "Z" as well as a few of those other difficult letters. Thumbing through my dictionary at this point just seemed like a tedious task.

I thought, too, that I might return to the meal metaphor I called forward in the opening section. I could ask you if you felt satiated, felt the meal was worth your time, or felt a need for second helpings. My sense, however, is that I already pushed that metaphor further than it ought to go, and even though I like closures that make a return to the beginning, sometimes they feel a bit too tidy.

Performance: An Alphabet of Performative Writing by Ronald J. Pelias, 207–208.

Finally, I considered talking about our relationship, about how we had a chance to stand face-to-face, how we might have given each other what the other needs, how our time together might have been meaningful. I would have mentioned how my reliance on performative writing may have brought us closer or kept us apart. I would have said that I hoped my language pulled you in, pulled you toward the subject and toward me. This closure also would have brought forward echoes from the beginning entry, placed an emphasis on the writer/reader relationship and the choices we have when we have an opportunity to come together. But such a strategy felt too presumptuous and too obvious at this point.

The decision I ultimately made was to offer just one more personal narrative, one final story that tells where I am. I have enjoyed writing this book and thinking about you in the process. After this long conversational turn I have taken, I am eager for your response. I feel I've learned quite a bit thinking about performance, putting ideas about performance into performative writing. For that reason alone, I am glad I spent the time with this project. It would be fun to start again, start from the beginning of the alphabet, but give myself one rule: Do not make any entries under the words that were used before. I wonder in what new ways would performance emerge, in what new ways would performative writing take form.

Entries by Subject

- Acting/Performing
  - Becoming
  - Knots
  - Rehearsal
  - Truth
- Creativity
  - Imagination
  - Language
  - Originality
- Everyday Life Performance
  - Imagination
  - Judgments
  - Justice
  - Naming
  - Stink
  - Ubiquitous
- Performance Criticism
  - Critical Responses
    - Confessions
    - Diminishments
    - Empathy
    - Insufficiency
    - Judgments
    - Memory
  - Critical Stances
    - Appreciation
    - Criticism
    - Epigraphs
    - Power
    - Quality
    - Reflexivity
    - Seduction
    - Sexuality
    - Stink
    - Taking
- Performance Pedagogy
  - Investments
  - Justice
- Performance Theory
  - Figure
  - Generative
  - Holy
  - Imagination
  - Insufficiency
  - Knots
  - Manifesto
  - Opening
  - Seduction
  - Sexuality
  - Vulnerable
  - Watching
  - Yearning
  - Zeitgeist
- Personal Narrative
  - Concealment
  - Confessions
  - Empathy
  - Pledge
  - Vulnerable
- Writing
  - Concealment
  - Devising
  - Language
  - Writing

References

Abrams, M. H. (1953). *The mirror and the lamp.* New York: Oxford University Press.

Alexander, B. K. (2000). *Skin Flint (or, The Garbage Man's Kid)*: A generative autobiographical performance based on Tami Spry's *Tattoo Stories. Text and Performance Quarterly 20*, 97–114.

Alexander, B. K., G. L. Anderson, and B. P. Gallegos (Eds.). (2005). *Performance theories in education: Power, pedagogy, and the politics of identity.* Malwah, NJ: Lawrence Erlbaum.

Bacon, W. A. (1972). *The art of interpretation*, 2nd ed. New York: Holt, Rinehart and Winston.

_____. (1976). A sense of being: Interpretation and the humanities. *Southern Speech Communication Journal 41*, 135–141.

Bakhtin, M. M. (1981). *The dialogic imagination.* Trans. C. Emerson and M. Holquist. Austin: University of Texas Press.

Barthes, R. (1977). *Image, music, text.* Trans. S. Heath. New York: Hill and Wang.

Baumeister, R. F., and L. S. Newman. (1994): How stories make sense of personal experiences: Motives that shape autobiographical narratives. *Personality and Social Psychology Bulletin 20*, 676–690.

Bell, E. (2008). *Theories of performance.* Thousand Oaks, CA: Sage.

Benjamin, W. (1979). *One-way street and other writings.* Trans. E. Jepcott and K. Shorter. London: New Left Books.

Bennett, S. (1990). *Theatre audiences: A theory of production and reception.* New York; Routledge.

Bogart, A. (2001). *A director prepares: Seven essays on art and theatre.* New York; Routledge.

Booth, P. (1989). Philip Booth: An interview by Rachel Berghash. *American Poetry Review 18*, 37–39.

Brecht, B. (1964). *Brecht on theatre*. Ed. J. Willett. New York: Hill and Wang.

Brook, C. (1947). *The well wrought urn: Studies in the structure of poetry*. New York: Harcourt, Bruce, and World.

Brook, P. (1968). *The empty space*. New York: Avon Books.

Burke, K. (1945). *A grammar of motives*. Englewood Cliffs, NJ: Prentice Hall.

Butler, J. (1990). *Gender trouble: Feminism and the subversion of identity*. New York: Routledge.

_____. (1993). *Bodies that matter: On the discursive limits of 'sex.'* New York: Routledge.

Buzard, J. (2003). On auto-ethnographic authority. *The Yale Journal of Criticism 16*, 61–91.

Canary, D. J., M. J. Cody, and V. L. Manusov. (2002). *Interpersonal communication: A goals-based approach*, 3rd ed. Boston: Bedford.

Carlson, M. (1990). *Theatre semiotics: Signs of life*. Bloomington: Indiana University Press.

Carr, C. (1993). On edge: Performance at the end of the twentieth century. Hanover, NH: Wesleyan University Press.

Clark, T. (1984). The end of the line. In *Paradise resisted: Selected poems 1978–1984*. Santa Barbara, CA: Black Sparrow Press.

Clifford, J. (1986). Introduction: Partial truths. In J. Clifford and G. E. Marcus (Eds.), *Writing culture: The poetics and politics of ethnography* (pp. 163–179). Berkeley: University of California Press.

Conquergood, D. (1995). Of caravans and carnivals. *The Drama Review 39*, 137–141.

_____. (2002). Performance studies: Inventions and radical research. *The Drama Review 46*, 145–156.

Crapanzano, V. (1986). Hermes dilemma: The making of subversion in ethnographic description. In J. Clifford and G. E. Marcus (Eds.), *Writing culture: The poetics and politics of ethnography* (pp. 51–76). Berkeley: University of California Press.

Deleuze, G., and F. Guattari. (1987). *A thousand plateaus: Capitalism and schizophrenia*. Trans. B. Massumi. Minneapolis: University of Minnesota Press.

Denzin, N. K. (1997). *Interpretive ethnography: Ethnographic practices for the 21st century.* Thousand Oaks, CA: Sage.

_____. (2003). *Performance ethnography: Critical pedagogy and the politics of culture.* Thousand Oaks, CA: Sage.

_____. (2006). The politics and ethics of performance pedagogy. In D. S. Madison and J. Hamera (Eds.), *The Sage handbook of performance studies* (pp. 325–338). Thousand Oaks, CA: Sage.

Derrida, J. (1976). *Of grammatology.* Trans. G. C. Spivak. Baltimore, MD: John Hopkins University Press.

Dobyns, S. (1996). Golden broilers. In *Common carnage.* New York: Penguin.

Dolan, J. (2001). Performance, utopia, and the 'utopian performative.' *Theatre Journal 53*, 455–479.

_____. (2005). *Utopia in performance: Finding hope at the theatre.* Ann Arbor: University of Michigan Press.

Dunn, S. (1994). Tenderness. In *New and selected poems 1974–1994.* New York: W. W. Norton.

_____. (1994). Loves. In *New and selected poems 1974–1994.* New York: W. W. Norton.

_____. (1994). Ordinary days. In *New and selected poems 1974–1994.* New York: W. W. Norton.

Eagleton, T. (1990). *The ideology of the aesthetic.* Oxford: Basil Blackwell.

Eakin, P. J. (1999). *How our lives become stories: Making selves.* Ithaca, NY: Cornell University Press.

Eco, U. (1976). *A theory of semiotics.* Bloomington: Indiana University Press.

Eliot, T. S. (1932/1964). Tradition and the individual talent. In *Selected essays of T. S. Eliot.* New York: Harcourt, Brace, and World.

Ellis, C. (1995). *Final negotiations: A story of love, loss, and chronic illness.* Philadelphia: Temple University Press.

Espinola, J. C. (1977). Oral interpretation performance: An act of publication. *Western Journal of Speech Communication 41*, 90–97.

Fassett, D. L., and J. T. Warren. (2007). *Critical communication pedagogy.* Thousand Oaks, CA: Sage.

Felman, S., and D. Laub. (1992). *Testimony: Crises of witnessing in literature, psychoanalysis, and history.* New York: Routledge.

Fisher, W. R. (1987). *Human communication as narration.* Columbia: University of South Carolina Press.

Forche, C. (1990). A TPQ interview: Jill Taft-Kaufman talks with Carolyn Forche. *Text and Performance Quarterly 10,* 61–70.

Fuoss, K. W. (1999). Lynching performances, theatres of violence. *Text and Performance Quarterly 19,* 1–37.

Gallagher, T. (1982). The poem as time machine. In D. Hall (Ed.), *Claims for poetry* (pp. 104–116). Ann Arbor: University of Michigan Press.

Garber, F. (1995). *Repositionings: Readings of contemporary poetry, photography, and performance art.* University Park: Pennsylvania State University Press.

Geertz, C. (1983). *Local knowledge.* New York: Basic Books.

Gingrich-Philbrook, C. (1998). Disciplinary violation: The stigmatized masculine voice of performance studies. *Communication Theory 8,* 203–220.

_____. (1998). What I 'know' about the story (for those about to tell personal narratives on stage). In S. J. Dailey (Ed.), *The future of performance studies: Visions and revisions,* (pp. 298–300). Annandale, VA: National Communication Association.

_____. (2–4 December, 1999). *Cups: Sufficiency enigma 1999.* Marion Kleinau Theatre, Southern Illinois University, Carbondale, IL.

_____. (2000). The personal and political in solo performance: Editor's introduction. *Text and Performance Quarterly 20,* vi–x.

Goffman, E. (1959). *The presentation of self in everyday life.* Garden City, NY: Doubleday.

Goodall, H. L., Jr. (1989). *Casing a promised land: The autobiography of an organizational detective as cultural ethnographer.* Carbondale: Southern Illinois University Press.

_____. (1991). *Living in the rock n roll mystery: Reading context, self, and others as clues.* Carbondale: Southern Illinois University Press.

_____. (1996). *Divine signs: Connecting spirit to community.* Carbondale: Southern Illinois University Press.

_____. (2000). *Writing the new ethnography.* Walnut Creek, CA: AltaMira.

Gordon, A. F. (1997). *Ghostly matters: Haunting and the sociological imagination.* Minneapolis: University of Minnesota Press.

Graver, D. (1997). The actor's bodies. *Text and Performance Quarterly 17,* 221–235.

Grotowski, J. (1968). *Towards a poor theatre.* New York: Simon and Schuster.

Gunn, J. (2006). Shittext: Toward a new coprophilic style." *Text and Performance Quarterly 26,* 79–97.

Hantzis, D. M. (1998). Reflections on "A dialogue with friends: 'Performing' the 'other'/ 'self' OJA 1995." In S. J. Dailey (Ed.), *The future of performance studies: Visions and revisions* (pp. 203–206). Annandale, VA: National Communication Association.

Hart, R. P. (1993). Why communication? Why education? Toward politics of teaching. *Communication Education 42,* 97–105.

Heaton, D. W. (1998). Twenty fragments: The 'other' gazing back or touring Juanita. *Text and Performance Quarterly 18,* 248–261.

Hirshfield, J. (2007). Poetry and the constellation of surprise. *The Writer's Chronicle 40,* 28–35.

Hoagland, T. (2003). Negative capability: How to talk mean and influence people. *American Poetry Review 32,* 13–15.

hooks, b. (1999) *Remembered rapture: The writer at work.* New York: Henry Holt.

Hudson, L. (1973). Oral interpretation as metaphoric expression. *Speech Teacher 22,* 27–31.

Johnson, D. W. (2009). Being open with and to other people. In J. Stewart (Ed.), *Bridges not walls,* 10th ed, (pp. 253–262). Boston: McGraw Hill.

Johnson, E. P. (2003). *Appropriating blackness: Performance and the politics of authenticity.* Durham, NC: Duke University Press.

Kershaw, B. (1999). *The radical in performance: Between Brecht and Baudrillard.* New York: Routledge.

Lamontt, A. (1994). *Bird by bird: Some instructions on writing and life.* New York: Anchor.

Langellier, K. M. (1998). Voiceless bodies, bodiless voices: The future of personal narrative performance. In S. J. Dailey (Ed.), *The future of performance studies: Visions and Revisions* (pp. 207–213). Annandale, VA: National Communication Association.

Langer, S. (1953). *Feeling and form.* New York: Charles Scribner's Sons.

Leder, D. (1990). *The absent body.* Chicago: University of Chicago Press.

Lockford, L. (2008). Investing in the political beyond. *Qualitative Inquiry 14*, 3–12.

Long, B. W., and M. F. HopKins. (1982). *Perfoming literature.* Englewood Cliffs, NJ: Prentice-Hall.

Lopate, P. (1996, September 8). Sans teeth. *The New York Times Book Review CI*, 39.

Madison, D. S. (1999). Performing theory/embodied writing. *Text and Performance Quarterly 19*, 107–124.

_____. (2005). *Critical ethnography: Method, ethics, and performance.* Thousand Oaks, CA: Sage.

_____. (2006). The dialogic performative in critical ethnography. *Text and Performance Quarterly 26*, 320–324.

McLaren, P. (1994). *Life in schools: An introduction to critical pedagogy in the foundations of education*, 2nd ed. White Plains, NY: Longman.

Miller, T., and D. Roman. (1995). Preaching to the choir. *Theatre Journal 47*, 169–188.

Munoz, J. E. (1999). *Disidentifications: Queers of color and the performance of politics.* Minneapolis: University of Minnesota Press.

Myers, W. B. (2012). The élan vital and sacred research: Questioning the spiritual imperative in performance studies. *Text and Performance Quarterly 32*, 162–174.

Owens, C. (1983). The discourse of others: Feminists and postmodernism. In H. Foster (Ed.), *The anti-aesthetic: Essays on postmodern culture* (pp. 57–82). Seattle, WA: Bay Press.

Park-Fuller, L., and T. Olsen. (1983). Understanding what we know: *Yonnondio: From the Thirties. Literature in Performance 4*, 65–77.

Parks, R. (1998). Where does scholarship begin? *American Communication Journal 1.* Retrieved October 1, 2002, from acjounal.org/holdings/vol1/ Iss2/ special/parks.htm

Pelias, R. J. (2004). *A Methodology of the heart: Evoking academic & daily life*. Walnut Creek, CA: AltaMira.

_____. (2008). Performative inquiry: Embodiment and its challenges. In J. G. Knowles and A. L. Coles (Eds.), *Handbook of the arts in qualitative inquiry: Perspectives, methodologies, examples, and issues* (pp. 185–193). Los Angeles: Sage.

Peterson, E., and K. Langelier. (1982). Creative double bind in oral interpretation. *Western Journal of Speech Communication 46*, 242–252.

Phelan, P. (1993). *Unmarked: The politics of performance.* New York: Routledge.

_____. (1997). *Mourning sex: Performing public memories.* New York: Routledge.

Pineau, E. L. (1995). Re-casting rehearsals: Making a case for production as research. *Journal of the Illinois Speech and Theatre Association 46*, 43–52.

_____. (2011). Intimacy, empathy, activism: A performative engagement with children's wartime art. In N. K. Denzin and M. D. Giardina (Eds.), *Qualitaitve inquiry and global crises* (pp. 199–217). Walnut Creek, CA: Left Coast Press, Inc.

Pollock, D. (1998). Writing performance. In P. Phelan and J. Lane (Eds.), *The ends of performance* (pp. 73–103). New York: New York University Press.

Powell, J. (1969). *Why am I afraid to tell you who I am?* Chicago: Argus Communications.

Roloff, L. H. (1973). *The perception and evocation of literature*. Glenview, IL: Scott, Foresman.

Schechner, R. (1985). *Between theatre & anthropology.* Philadelphia: University of Pennsylvania Press.

_____. (1993). *The future of ritual: Writings on culture and performance.* New York: Routledge.

Scholes, R. (1992). Response. *Text and Performance Quarterly 12*, 75–78.

Searle, J. R. (1969). *Speech acts: An essay in the philosophy of language.* Cambridge: Cambridge University Press.

Sheets-Johnstone, M. (1990). *The roots of thinking.* Philadelphia: Temple University Press.

Smith, A. D. (1993). *Fires in the mirror.* New York: Doubleday.

_____. (2000). *Twilight: Los Angeles, 1992.* New York: Random House.

Smith, R. E. (1998). A personal look at personal narratives. In S. J. Dailey (Ed.), *The future of performance studies: Visions and revisions,* (pp. 207–213). Annandale, VA: National Communication Association.

Spry, T. (2011). *Body, paper, stage: Writing and performing autoethnography.* Walnut Creek, CA: Left Coast Press, Inc.

Stafford, K. (2003). *The muses among us.* Athens: University of Georgia Press.

States, B. O. (1996). Performance as metaphor. *Theatre Journal 48,* 1–26.

Steiner, W. (1995). *The scandal of pleasure.* Chicago: University of Chicago Press.

Strine, M. S., B. W. Long, and M. F. HopKins. (1990). Research in interpretation and performance studies. In G. M. Phillips and J. T. Wood (Eds.), *Speech communication: Essays to commemorate the 75th anniversary of the Speech Communication Association* (pp. 181–204). Carbondale: Southern Illinois University Press.

Taylor, J. (1987). Documenting performance knowledge: Two narrative techniques in Grace Paley's fiction. *Southern Speech Communication Journal 53,* 65–79.

Terry, D. P. (2006). Once blind, now seeing: Problematics of confessional performance. *Text and Performance Quarterly 26,* 209–228.

Trinh, Minh-ha T. (1991). *When the moon waxes red: Representation, gender and cultural politics.* New York: Routledge.

Turner, V. (1974). *Dramas, fields, and metaphors: Symbolic action in human society.* Ithaca, NY: Cornell University Press.

_____. (1982). *From ritual to theatre: The human seriousness of play.* New York: Performing Arts Press.

Tyler, A. (1986). Post-modern ethnography: From document of the occult to occult document. In J. Clifford and G. E. Marcus (Eds.), *Writing culture: The poetics and politics of ethnography* (pp. 122–140). Berkeley: University of California Press.

Webb, C. H. (2011). How do they do it?: The power poems of B. H. Fairchild and Dorianne Laux. *The Writer's Chronicle 44.2*, 32–42.

Wendt, T. A. (1998). The ways and means of knowing: The 'problem' of scholarship in a postmodern world. *American Communication Journal 1.* Retrieved October 1, 2002, from acjounal.org/holdings/vol1/Iss2/ special/ wendt.htm

Wilson, K. (2011). *The family Fang.* New York: Ecco.

Woodruff, P. (2008). *The necessity of theatre: The art of watching and being watched.* Oxford: Oxford University Press.

Zingaro, L. (2009). *Speaking out: Storytelling for social change.* Walnut Creek, CA: Left Coast Press, Inc..

Author's Index

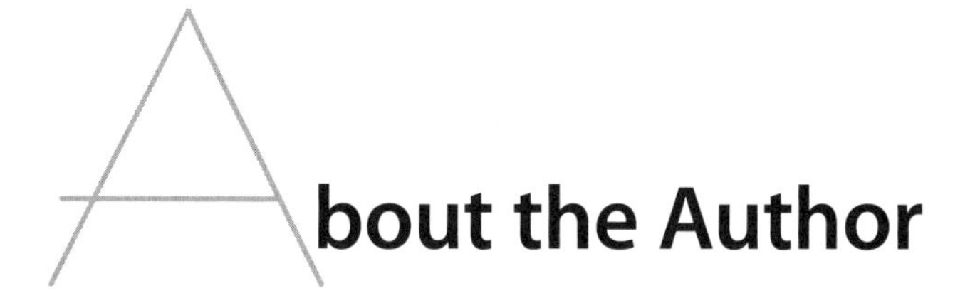

About the Author

Ronald J. Pelias is a professor emeritus in the Department of Speech Communication at Southern Illinois University, Carbondale. He is the author of numerous books on performance studies and performance methodologies, including *Writing Performance: Poeticizing the Researcher's Body* (Southern Illinois University Press, 1999), *A Methodology of the Heart: Evoking Academic and Daily Life* (AltaMira, 2004), *Performance Studies: The Interpretation of Aesthetic Texts, 2e* (Kendall Hunt, 2007) with Tracy Stephenson Shaffer, and *Leaning: A Poetics of Personal Relations* (Left Coast, 2011). In 2000, he received the Lilla A. Heston Award for Outstanding Scholarship in Interpretation and Performance Studies from the National Communication Association. In addition to numerous published articles and book chapters, he also publishes performance texts and poetry.

Left Coast Press, Inc. is committed to preserving ancient forests and natural resources. We elected to print this title on 30% post consumer recycled paper, processed chlorine free. As a result, for this printing, we have saved:

2 Trees (40' tall and 6-8" diameter)
1 Million BTUs of Total Energy
157 Pounds of Greenhouse Gases
848 Gallons of Wastewater
56 Pounds of Solid Waste

Left Coast Press, Inc. made this paper choice because our printer, Thomson-Shore, Inc., is a member of Green Press Initiative, a nonprofit program dedicated to supporting authors, publishers, and suppliers in their efforts to reduce their use of fiber obtained from endangered forests.

For more information, visit www.greenpressinitiative.org

Environmental impact estimates were made using the Environmental Defense Paper Calculator. For more information visit: www.papercalculator.org.